The People's History

Our Village

Memories Of The Durham Mining Communities

Edited by

Keith Armstrong

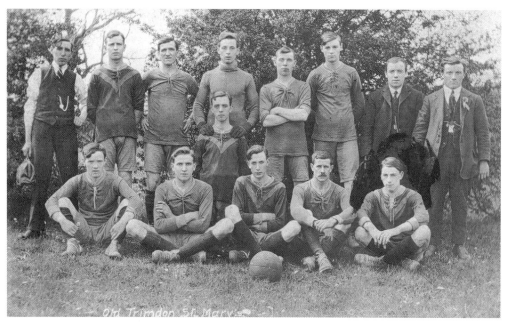

Old Trimdon St Mary's football team.

Previous page: Ryhope Prize Band in 1929.

Copyright © Northern Voices 2000

First published in 2000 by

The People's History Ltd
Suite 1
Byron House
Seaham Grange Business Park
Seaham
Co. Durham
SR7 0PY

ISBN 1 902527 32 1

Contents

The Blue Stone, Sherburn.

This Village

This village draws me,
I hear it calling me back through the years.
Its people are its life blood,
I am its joys, I am its tears.

Makers were forged here
To forge a bond no cruel hands could destroy.
Artists' hands seized it, lost lovers grieved for it,
Builders have reached for its skies,
Poets have captured its beauty,
They speak of its sad beauty now.

This village haunts me,
Its whispering hurt tears at my soul.
Oh why did I forsake you?
Welcome me back, welcome me home.

A sacred bond exists here
Between the land and the people it owns.
It grants no escape from the realms of its fate,
It reaps the crops we have sown,
This village has made me all that I am,
This village is calling me home.

Gary Miller of 'The Whisky Priests'
from the album *Life's Tapestry*

Introduction

This book reflects the pains and joys of the people of the Durham Coalfield during a period of drastic change. It is a selection from a series of community publications I have been involved in over the last 20 years or so, from the 'Strong Words' series to the booklets of 'Durham Voices' and, now, 'Northern Voices'.

The general idea behind all these projects has been to let the people speak for themselves in conversation and in their songs and poems.

Mixed with vivid photographs of their local communities, what comes across is a passionate, and often agonising, account of the social upheaval Durham has experienced since the 1970s when we began publishing.

There is gloom aplenty but also wit and vitality in what people have to say. From the banks of the Derwent to the Weardale hills, from the beaches of Easington to proud Westoe, they tell their tales and laugh and cry.

Not everyone featured here has survived to celebrate the publication. Bearing this in mind, I hope that both text and pictures will interest and enthuse young and old and keep the fires of heritage burning at a crucial period of our social history. If that heritage is to survive outside of museums, we need to listen to these voices of hardened experience as well as to the songs of the young and, in by doing so, reclaim the values of solidarity, collective action and community.

Keith Armstrong
2000

Ferryhill Town Hall.

VILLAGE LIVES

Seaside Lane, Easington Colliery. The imposing building on the right is the old Primary School closed in the 1990s. It was replaced by a 'state of the art' school in Whickham Street.

Canny Old Soul, My Ma

A canny old soul was my ma. I loved her during the depression years as a kid. In a family of seven I was the seventh and it was 'hand to mouth' for us.

The fish cart would come round and ma would go out and get a dishful of herrings about 1d a piece, and boy could my ma cook. When the rising loaves of bread were laid out on the fender, ready to go into the oven, ma would give me the fork to stick each one, two, three or four times. Getting that oven hot was like setting a blast furnace away. Everything went under it, old boots, clogs, shoes, lumps of wood – anything that burnt. Fireplaces, in those days, had a back burner so it was one pailful on, one at the back and one standing.

Ma kept the mangle in the kitchen. It was kept in a recess in the wall, and when not in use ma would cover it over with a cloth. The dripping board used to stick out a bit and she would put something on there and it looked like a prize piano covered up. Ma had, as we say, all her buttons on.

She always paid for her things as she got them. The rent was always put on the corner of the mantelpiece. The insurance money (we were all insured for 1d a week) was always kept on the stairs. The doctor's man was about 1/6d a fortnight. Once a week, ma would send me to the local shop for a quarter pound of best butter. This cost 2$^{1}/_{2}$d. Then she said: 'When you lot are nicely in bed, I am going to treat myself.'

One day I came back from the shop and said: 'Mam, those other kids

Slake Terrace, Cornforth.

Front Street, Pelton Fell.

(mentioning their names) get all sorts and the man just puts it in a book until Friday.'

'Yes,' ma said, 'and when the bill comes round there is all sorts down that you haven't had. How do you think they (the shopkeepers) can afford to live in the big house?' Ma seemed to know all the answers.

She kept a stone jar in the oven. It was filled with barley, the rest with water. She made us drink it because she said it was good for our kidneys. It was the same tale when she took me for a pair of trousers. They would come almost underneath my armpits. 'Keep your kidneys warm,' she would say.

Ma used to send me to the butchers every Saturday night to get a basket of bones. She made a big pan of broth with them. I was like the 'Bisto Kid' waiting until I got a plateful. Then I sat on the bottom of the stairs and enjoyed every bit of it.

We used to get milk from the farm. Mother used to send up to the farm to get a big enamel jug full of old milk. I always thought it was left over from the day before, but as it happens it was milk which has had all the cream taken off it. It cost 1½d. If there was none I'd have to buy a gill of new, which hardly covered the bottom of the jug. Mother used to make all sorts of puddings – bread puddings, rice puddings, you name it, she made it. I also had to get a half a stone of crushed oatmeal. The farmer would just dig his pail into a heap of loose oats in his warehouse – rats and mice probably running over it – put it through his machine and it came out oatmeal. Ma would bake some brown bread and we ate and enjoyed every bit of it. Years later I had to tell the dentist the reason why I was forever breaking my false teeth – my mother encouraged me to eat up all my crusts.

The threshing machine would pull into the farmyard in the autumn and as soon as us kids heard its humming sound, off we went. The men threw the sheaves of corn from the stack on to the thresher, then women picked them up and cut the string and fed it into the machine. We stood around the stack with sticks catching all the mice that ran out. At dinner time the farmer's wife would come out with a big bag of sandwiches and tea and the men and women would sit in the big barn to eat it. They got about five or six shillings a day. Ma always made me empty my pockets when I got back. I had once bought a mouse home. It emerged, and it was weeks before father caught it. I never heard the end of it. I used to like watching the huge traction engine with the big wheel buzzing around with a big long belt attached, driving the thresher and the man poking the fire up now and then.

Hygiene seemed a bit different in those days. Ma wore her hair in long plaits. She would comb it, plait it, then coil it at the back of her head. I thought she looked a Queen. Father and I had different ideas about my hair. He used to sit me outside in the yard, get the scissors, take one of ma's pudding basins and plonk it on my head, then he'd

A typical colliery coal cart in the Ryhope/Silksworth area. Known as 'coop' carts, because they tipped over. 'Coop' was a local dialect word meaning to tip over. To 'coop one's creels' was to turn head-over-heals – a popular playground bit of showmanship.

The Bell Hotel, Horden. 8488

The Bell Hotel, Horden.

cut around it. Ma always bought bars of blue mottle soap, mostly to do the washing with. She cut a slice off for us and it was awful, more for taking the skin off you than the dirt. The towels we used were made by ma out of sugar bags from the 'Home and Colonial Stores'.

The kitchen was distempered pink with the ceiling whitewashed, the bedrooms were the same with a gas tap in the corner. The beds had all steel lathes underneath and straw mattress on top. Ma kept all the bits of soap leftovers and put them in a stone jar, then she made soft soap out of it for washing in the poss-tub. The poss-tub was the main item in everyone's yard and the poss-stick always stood in the corner of the 'netty' as the toilet was called. The poss-tub man would call shouting 'poss-tubs to mend'. He would have some hoops over his shoulder to repair any broken ones on ma's poss-tub. The rag and bone man, with his horse and cart, went all round the back streets shouting into the backyards of the houses: 'Scouring stone!' 'Rags and bones!' People would give him whatever they had to spare and he would give them some scouring stone in return. It made the doorway quite nice.

Now and then an epidemic would break out. Someone had smallpox or chicken pox or the fever, then the fever van would come around and take the affected people to hospital. The fever van was just like a caravan with no windows on the sides, and the door at the back. We all kept clear of that. A lot of people had consumption at that time. Whole families died of it.

Cornforth Lane, Coxhoe.

As kids we were for ever having boils, mostly on the neck, although some people could not sit down for them. Father, in his homely way, used to make a bread poultice with hot water and place it on my neck. I would howl the house down, next day it seemed like a half a loaf of bread was around your neck. It would nicely heal up, then another one would come. Talk about the good old days!

In those days people kept their own pigs and they often had them killed in their backyards. They would put a cabbage leaf down for it to eat, then hit it on the head with a wooden mallet, cut its throat then roll it into the bath tin where hot water was poured over it and it was scraped clean. Us kids waited until we got its bladder, blew it up like a balloon, and that was our football for the day.

There was a slaughterhouse between our house and the old school and, when the man was ready to kill a beast, he would put the rope around its neck, put the other end through a ring in the floor and then tell us kids to pull for all our worth. The beast would be pulled down to the ring, then the man with a pole axe would finally finish it off. It was done in front for everyone to see, doors wide open with us kids stretched out on the rope. We enjoyed every minute of it. I used to go back at night time with my little barrow to get offal; father said it was very good for his leeks.

Dick Beavis

Dipton – known as the 'long village'.

Church Street, Coxhoe.

Colliery Rows

The colliery rows, houses with one large downstairs kitchen and one garret bedroom, reached by ladder-like stairs, were in close streets with the doors opening straight on the road. Parents slept downstairs, often in four poster beds facing the door, and, when there was a death in the house, the corpse was laid on the trestles at the foot of the bed.

Mother used to have a wood tub or zinc bath waiting on the mat and a pan and kettle of water on the fire for her man's daily bath in front of a roaring fire. These fires were kept burning night and day, and the round colliery ovens were always warm, with the hearth and underbars whitewashed every day.

I remember being told by my grandmother that, when she came to Trimdon as a bride in 1830, she was astounded that there was not even an individual toilet in the street, Railway Row, and her husband had to build one in order to keep his wife.

The regular plan of every kitchen was a square eating table with an oilcloth under the window plus a wooden form for seating, and a round table in the centre. On this table there was a plush cover with the family bible in the centre surmounted by a globe of wax fruits. The big press in the corner was covered with a white crochet edged cloth and portraits in gilt frames were displayed everywhere. The now fashionable china dogs and two large ornaments and brass candlesticks adorned the mantle, a brass line ran underneath for drying clothes and the rest was enlivened by a high steel fender and massive irons. Pokers

Coffee Pot Street, Trimdon Colliery. There are a number of versions of how the street got its name. It is said that a Mr Walker had a coffee pot hanging outside his shop in the street or that the old pit engine looked like a coffee pot.

A general view of Kelloe.

had to be long in those days, for fireplaces were deep set and often took five buckets of coals. A cracket always stood near the fire and a rocking chair. Fridays were nightmare days when all brass and steel had to be cleaned and placed on the round table until the Saturday. Everybody aimed to make a new hooky or prodded mat for Christmas and special neighbours all went to help each other with work and clippings. When all was done, and the mat was got out, a huge pan of toffee was put on to boil for celebrations.

Water had to be carried from a communal tap in the street and the women went with their buckets to get steam water from the pit for their weekly wash. This was done by tub and poss-stick, double possing being done by two people who kept the rhythm going.

At one time, the dead were laid out with great honour, having white sheets over a clothes horse for a screen, which was trimmed with huge mauve satin ribbons. Bidders had wide mauve or white sashes draped over their shoulders and they set off to knock at everybody's door. When it was answered they said: 'Mrs So and So invites you to the funeral on Monday. Gather at two, lift at three.' On the day of the funeral six chairs would be placed outside the door, the coffin put on top and everybody would sing hymns over it in the street. They all walked in procession (wearing deep mourning) to the place of worship and thence to the churchyard which was often Kelloe, a few miles distant. Everybody returned to the house for a farewell feast of ham and pease pudding. It was a disgrace if you could not be buried with ham.

Eveline Johnson

St Michael & All Angels Church, Esh.

Frank Atkinson, in his book, *Life And Traditions in Northumberland And Durham*, used the recollections of George Bell of Bishop Auckland, a former miner born in 1884 to give a vivid account of a life in a pit village. Here he records the diet of a mining family:

'Pot-pies were very popular as were rabbit pies made from fresh wild rabbits which cost a shilling a couple. Ham and egg pies, girdle cakes and oven cakes were all good substantial food, as were various kinds of boiled puddings such as spotted dick, suet dumplings and treacle dumplings. Large teacakes were often made with plenty of currants in them, not one or two now! And fresh herring could be bought at twenty for a penny from fish hawkers every week in the season. There were of course no electric ovens then and the coal-fired oven, whether round or square, had to cook everything.

Milk was a penny a pint and could be got from the nearest farm. It was a job which the children had to do before going to school in the morning and sometimes the evening as well. Old milk could be bought for a penny a quart and many housewives used this when baking bread. Naturally no-one bought bread in those days. Flour was bought by the stone and kept in a large bin in the pantry, where the house had one, or otherwise in any convenient corner.'

An Esh Village Childhood

Esh lies on a ridge of land that runs between the Browney Valley on the north and the Deerness Valley to the south. I was born there and when I was young the village consisted of a long main street known as Front Street, the houses of which were un-numbered. The main shop in the village was the 'the store', ie the Co-op. This was, in those days, a favourite meeting place for the women of the village. I used to go there with my mother and must say that, far from being bored with the waiting, I was entertained by the company. There was the proud looking old lady who used to boast that she had never had a headache in her life and used to seem rather contemptuous of women who did have headaches.

Then there was the family all of whose members were stricken by bow-leggedness – rickets, I suppose, but I knew nothing of that then. There was too, an old woman, wrinkled, weatherbeaten and possessing the ugliest teeth I have ever seen: normally hidden, they would protrude like witch's fangs when she opened her mouth; and yet it was never frightening to see her. She was a hard-working spinster who made a living, together with her sister, by keeping hens and making pikelets. She used to tramp the roads around Esh selling these pikelets, and I have heard of her being encountered many miles away from home on her 'rounds'. These two sisters used to keep their hens in a corner of a small field owned by the local Catholic Church. The parish priest allowed them to have this land quite free. His successor refused to let them occupy it with their hens, a fact which must have seemed most un-Christian to many of his parishioners.

Jack Goundry

The post office at Esh.

Esh Village which lies between the Browney Valley and Deerness Valley.

Lodgers, Pigs And Gardens

I was born in Mersey Street, Chopwell. I was born into a family of eight brothers and seven sisters. My dad was a miner all his life. But that wasn't all; he was a breeder of pigs and my mother used to keep lodgers. She was just a little woman who used to do all her own baking and all her own washing. She'd look after anybody in the street that happened to be pregnant, taking the men meals in when they were coming in from the pit and so on. She used to run up and down the streets with white cloths over a steaming hot dinner ready for the man coming in from the pit. That was a tradition then with most women – a man coming in from the pit must have a good hot dinner. My dad used to always say that if you got one good meal a day you would take no hurt after that.

We had lodgers, pigs and gardens. We used to come in from school after playing marbles and my father would shout: 'Hey, feed the pigs!' And after you'd fed the pigs you would have to go and seek horse muck; following the horses around!

My dad worked in the colliery and we lived in a normal sized four-roomed colliery house. Sitting room, kitchen, two bedrooms and a small kitchenette with a tap on the wall and everywhere home-made mats on the floor. We used to have a pig lying on the pantry floor. We used to kill our own pigs of course and we used to cure them. We used to go to the store and get a big block of salt and rub the salt into the pig and it would lie six weeks. Then you turned it over and you did the same the other side. Then it was cured and ready for eating. We used to have legs of ham and we used to hang them from big hooks in the ceiling.

My mother used to have a big round frying pan. It used to take the whole fireplace up – the old fashioned fireplace. She'd fry big slices of beef. We used to get the old stotty cake out and dip our bread in the juice. There used to be flakes of brown meat on the bottom of the pan. We would dip our stotty cake into the pan and the grease used to be running down your chin. There used to be a pot at the side of the old fireplace and we used to half fill it with broth, leak soup, turnips, carrots, potatoes and peas and then a piece of ham was hoyed in. That was our house.

George Alsop

Derwent Street, Chopwell.

The Mother & The Spider

Writing about my mother brings back some memories. One was the day she gave a man a good hiding. I was about three or four and my elder brother was playing outside with some mates when he ran in holding his neck. The man two doors away for some reason had tried to choke my brother. My mother was hot-tempered and went outside and gave this chap a good 'scudding'.

Later in the day, a policeman knocked on our door stating that the person wanted to press charges for an assault and battery. My mother said: 'Look at my bairn's neck.' He looked and went to see the man.

They both had to go to Castle Eden court and my mother wouldn't shut up. 'Nobody touches my bairns,' she kept on shouting. Both were

Deaf Hill, Trimdon. The colliery was sunk at Deaf Hill in 1870 by the Trimdon Coal Co. It closed in the 1960s.

bound over to keep the peace but the old lady was later told she would have won her case if she had kept her head.

The case was a laughing stock because it had never been heard of a man bringing a woman up for assault and battery rather than the other way round. If the man thought that was the end of the matter he was to find out otherwise.

Some time later, mother was going to the fish shop with an enamel tureen in her hand. Now the chippy was set on some wasteground with no street lights on hand. This man came out of the chippy and into the darkness outside where he was momentarily blinded. He became more blinded when mother swung her arm and hit him with the tureen. He never found out yet who stunned him.

One old-timer named Dick Rickaby lived in a hut near the 'Locomotive' at Trimdon Colliery and the old 'Burton Hotel'. He must have been a hard man living in those conditions. Oil lamp and water butt were the sources of lighting and washing for this old-timer.

Another character was 'Spider Wood' who lived in a caravan and wore a patch over one eye. I was only a bairn but I can still remember him vaguely. Ned Scully was another character who kept ducks, hens and goats. He had a house full of kids and one tale goes that a man went and asked Ned if he had any cabbages for sale. The reply was 'yes' and when the man went to Ned's house one Sunday morning for a cabbage he asked how much he wanted. Ned said: 'Just give the bairns a copper or two.' But when the man saw all the kids it dawned on him that it was an expensive cabbage!

The Lowe family were another laugh with some queer tales. The father was called Matt and was nicknamed 'Crock'. He worked on the screens or aerial flight at Deaf Hill Colliery. One night Matt had gone out for a drink and must have gone over the eight. He collapsed in the yard and it was teeming with rain. Someone passing the yard went and knocked on the door and when Mrs Lowe answered she was told: 'Mrs Lowe, your Matt's lying in the yard.'

She replied: 'Just put it over the wall and it will dry out in the morning.'

John Iddon

Middle Street, Blackhall

Middle Street, Blackhall.

At The Top Of The Bank

I was born in Station Town, Wingate. I had three sisters and three brothers. The boys had one bedroom and the girls the other. My father belonged Wingate and my mother belonged Sacriston – she played first violin in the Sacriston Orchestra. They were married at Wingate and then they went to Blackhall and to Shotton and finally to Trimdon. We lived in the first house at the top of the bank. I was brought up there from the age of 10.

From seventeen years old, my dad worked down the pit at Shotton

Front Street, Wingate. The most famous man to work at Wingate Colliery was Peter Lee who became General Secretary of the Durham Miners' Association.

Colliery. He had a heart attack and at the age of 22 he was advised to get out of the pit straight away and he managed to get an Attendance Officer's job (School Board Man) for the Trimdon area.

We were all brought up staunch Methodists. My father was a Methodist preacher. There was father, mother and the seven of us in the choir at the old Methodist Chapel in Trimdon Village.

Peter Lee, the Durham Miners' leader, was my half uncle. My grandmother married twice and her first husband was Peter Lee's brother, Jack Lee. Peter Lee used to come to our house when he lectured. I can remember him quite distinctly. My father and he were really good friends.

We had two days washing – one for the whites and one for the coloureds. I don't know how they coped in those days with the poss-tub and poss-stick. I had a poss-stick and my mother had a poss-stick and I stood on a cracket – when she came up, I went down. And we had two days of ironing – and that was at the age of 10, you know. We all had our own jobs to do. As the oldest girl I had a lot of slogging to do, but I was never unhappy. I can never remember being unhappy.

Rachel Ord

An unmade-up street in Shotton.

Hope Street, Crook.

Shy Bairns Get Nee Broth
(in memory of Billy Horn of Shotton Colliery)

Shy bairns get nee broth,
shy bairns get nee broth,
so don't be scared to do your worst,
'cos shy bairns get nee broth.

I met an old miner in the club,
he was leaning on his life.
He dragged his way through a burnt-out day,
and this is what he coughed, he coughed:

Shy bairns get nee broth,
shy bairns get nee broth,
so don't be scared to do your worst,
'cos shy bairns get nee broth.

His face glowed in the village gloom,
as another short went down.
His eyes gleamed and his tongue it wagged,
and these wise words just flowed, he cried:

Shy bairns get nee broth,
shy bairns get nee broth,
so don't be scared to do your worst,
'cos shy bairns get nee broth.

He shone through the clatter of the dominoes,
with a song inside his heart.
He danced in the bar-light from his head to his toes;
there was life in the old dog yet; he sang:

Shy bairns get nee broth,
shy bairns get nee broth,
so don't be scared to do your worst,
'cos shy bairns get nee broth.

There came a year when he'd had enough
and life just seeped out of him.
There's a space in the club where he used to sit
and, above it, there's this sign, it says:

Shy bairns get nee broth,
shy bairns get nee broth,
so don't be scared to do your worst,
'cos shy bairns get nee broth.

Keith Armstrong

Blind Lane, Silksworth, in the 1950s. The Miners' Hall is in the centre. Like many former halls and institutes, since the demise of its local colliery it no longer has an important role in the village.

Whitewashed colliery houses at Ryhope. The photograph was taken from the pit heap and the colliery is in the foreground.

The Social Club at Chopwell.

Back Kitchens

All my family were leadminers. I was three-and-a-half when we came to Leadgate with my mother. She had come to keep house for a chap. He was a blacksmith and eventually he became my stepfather. So I was fetched up in that house. It was called the 'back kitchens'. It was one up and one down and you went upstairs through a ladder; there wasn't staircases then. Eleven of us children were fetched up there.

My stepfather had started at the pit when he was nine. His mother used to carry him over to the Busty Pit. He was married three times. His first wife died in childbirth, I think, and then he married her sister. And she died.

There were three streets of 'back kitchens' in Leadgate. They'd been improved by taking off the coalhouses and such, like off the back and building on a back kitchen. The toilets were just earth closets – open ash heaps – and when I went to work at the Eden Colliery the first colliery house I had was that type. Outside there was an open drainage system. There was a common channel that came down the back and there would be a sink half way down and one at the bottom. They were always a bone of contention and people would often fall out. People wouldn't wash their share of the gutter until people above them had washed theirs. I've seen women tearing the hair out of each other over these gutters.

Tommy Armstrong, the pitman poet who lived at Stanley, wrote a song about these quarrels. There were about half a dozen verses like this:

> One day I went walking
> I heard some folk talking
> With voices as loud as the one o'clock gun
> And though I could hear them
> I couldn't get near them
> For folks of all kind were enjoying the fun.

Fenwick Whitfield

Front Street, Leadgate.

Grange Terrace Days

I was born in number 20 Grange Terrace, Pelton, in 1917. My father worked at the pit head but left in 1937 to go to Horden. I was brought up with an aunt in number 14 Grange Terrace because my mother died when I was six months old. My parents had five children and I was the youngest one.

My grandmother died at that particular time and my mother was having me – it was even harder work having a baby in those days – she got out of bed too soon to go to the funeral and she took pneumonia and died.

My father lived in number 27 Grange Terrace and my grandmother in number 67 so we were a tight-knit family.

The schoolmaster was a chap called Mr Legg, I didn't start until I was six and I went there until I was twelve. Then I was transferred to the Roseberry School. I remember young lads going to school in their bare feet with frost on the ground. To get there you had to go down a great big bank and over an old bridge. Sometimes the old bridge was washed away and Mr Harvey, the schoolteacher, used to carry us over to get to the school. There were no school meals so we used to have to go back home again for lunch – up and down the bank.

I remember the Prince of Wales visiting Newfield. He went to North View. At that time, the people used to make stotty cakes and put them on the front or back to cool. The Prince was amazed to see them.

During the 1926 Strike I used to go over to the old tip and dig for bottles. When I found one, I used to take it home and wash it out. I took them to the Top House and got a penny a bottle. Then I went to the fish shop and got a bag of chips. I was just nine years old.

Joe Glassey

The Colliery Inn, Front Street, Pelton Fell.

Coal And Life

I was born in Bankfoot Cottages near Crook, they are down now and it is all back to agricultural land. In the early days, they found coal there and coal needs workers. The coal owners were mainly concerned how to get the people in to produce the coal. There was one row of over a hundred houses. That was Wooley Terrace, two rows of fifty houses with a break in the middle. Local gossip had it that the quickest way of communication was tapping on the fire back. The fire places were back to back and the messages could go right down the row.

Market Place, Crook. 1557.

These houses had no bathrooms of course and the toilets were across the road. There were no 'mod cons'. We used to have an earth closet and the farmers would clean them out and use it as fertiliser. There was a lot of illness. In those days it was accepted that people would have TB, diphtheria and scarlet fever.

We had two allotments both of which had vegetables in. Potatoes and greens were the main source of food – especially if you were like my father who had two boys at home. The only thing in the house garden was rhubarb and that was in the house for my mother. The main staple was potatoes. When a chap had been down the pit six days a week he needed fresh air and he could go out on his allotment.

My father died when the colliery was still working and I was left with my mother. She knew that she would eventually have to leave the house but the company didn't push her out straight away. They weren't that bad, they would give her time. Once the man died, the company would assist the widow to find another house so another worker could move in. In a sense it was like a tied cottage. But it so happened that a house came empty at High Grange, a small village of sixty-five houses, where she used to work in service. My mother went into service when she was thirteen and this was an acceptable job for a girl in those days. She would work for the local gentry, starting by scrubbing floors in the kitchen. Anyway, she knew this house and so we were able to move out of Bankfoot within three or four weeks of my father dying.

Arthur Turnbull

Front Street, Wingate.

Leeches And Maggots

I was born in Pitt Street, Thornley. I was the youngest of six, two bothers and four sisters. My father was a miner all his working life. My mother was a shop assistant before she married. The pit head ran along the bottom of the street.

My grandparents on my father's side came from South Shields when they were young. My grandfather was a miner, my grandfather bred leeches and maggots for the local doctors, the leeches to draw blood, the maggots for putrid flesh such as gangrene. She came from a seafaring family, her father was a sea captain and her brothers were seamen. She was a bit of an outcast because she married a miner.

My grandparents on my mother's side came from Cumberland, my grandfather was a miner and was involved with the unions as was his eldest son. They were both blacklisted at several collieries because of union activities. My grandmother was midwife for Thornley, Wheatley Hill and Ludworth. She had her diploma with the wax seal and ribbon hung above her bed. Her brown Gladstone bag was at the side of her bed in case she was called out during the night. People gave her old sheets and pillow cases and my mother and her sisters made baby gowns, barracoats and binders for the poorer families. My grandmother took them with her when she was called to deliver babies. When she died in 1946, aged 87, I read her births' register. In the margin, by the side of some of the births, was DB in red ink, this meant dead born. There was quite a lot.

Gladys Bromlow

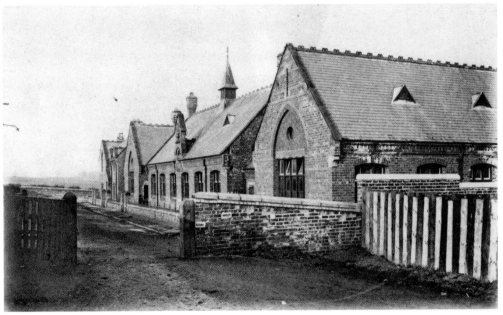

Thornley Schools. In the 19th century, schools were often supported by the colliery owners who would provide buildings and annual grants. At Thornley provision was also made for a Catholic school.

High Speed Teacher

There's one schoolteacher that stands out in my memory. She came to school on a motorbike, dressed in brown leathers, flying jacket, trousers, helmet and goggles. She looked like a First World War pilot, then she'd walk into assembly looking smart in a tweed skirt and twin set.

Gladys Bromilow

Two photographs taken by renowned railway photographer Ian S. Carr. Ian has chronicled the changing face of industry in the North East. His images record many railways, mines, shipyards and factories which have now gone. Above: One of the many trains that would make the daily journey from Tyne Dock to Consett carrying iron ore to the steelworks. This train is between Washington and West Boldon in 1966. The line closed a few months later. Below: This engine heads a coke train through Brancepeth in 1962. Brancepeth lost its regular passenger service in 1964.

Thornley. Like many colliery villages the population of the area exploded with the introduction of mining. In 1801 just over 50 people lived in the small hamlet. Sixty years later the population was over 3,300.

Fishburn Days

I was born at Horse Shoe Cottage, at the top of Salter's Lane, Fishburn. My mother was born in, and eventually died in, the same room. Her father was William Garbutt, he was woodsman at Galleylaw. The hounds used to meet at the cottage, in the charge of Squire Ord. Lord and Lady Londonderry were always at the Meet. The Three Horse Shoes public house was nearby, and at one time there was a butcher's shop. The animals were killed and the meat was taken out by butcher's cart by Bill Reed. One day a patient from the Asylum hung himself in the cart shed. It was also struck by lightning twice.

All the water we needed was carried from Bridge House Farm, two pailfuls at a time. You can imagine what it was like on a washing day. If we wanted to go to Stockton we had to walk to Wynyard Station, and to get to Darlington we had to walk to Bradbury or Ferryhill. Many farmers' wives from the small farms, my mother also, all walked to Stockton or Durham carrying baskets of eggs and butter.

There was a lovely big house in Fishburn called Fishburn Hall, it was near the crossroads. The iron gates were made of iron hung from two big pillars, with a fancy carved piece on the top. The hall and the staircase were all of carved wood and I think it was a shame that it was disposed of. I heard that it went to America, at least that's what we were told.

Trimdon House was over Fishburn Moors and my cousin worked

Park View, Fishburn. 3780

Beehive Inn, Park View, Fishburn.

there as a cook. It was said that it was haunted. In one of the bedrooms a ghost always left a trail over the floor as if someone had just stepped out of the bath. It was once a boys' school.

Dances were often held in farmers' barns especially after harvest time. Many is the time we've walked to Wynyard Hall Farm, Stillington, or to Dove's Farm at Bishop Middleham. A lot of people of my age will remember the old Church School. All the children from the out-lying farms had to walk miles to get there. Their parents could not afford the time to bring them. I often wonder what became of the big stone that stood outside the school at the gates. One day my brother and two other boys, Charles Hirst and Fred Collinson, had played truant and, when they had gone back to school, the teacher sent them out for a big stone to knock some sense into them. So they went and rolled this big stone right into the middle of the classroom then took off again. Next morning they got the cane and were told to put the stone back to exactly where they got it from.

Work was hard in those days. If you didn't get to work at any of the big houses in the district, you just got to work as a farm hand doing the same work as a man did. I remember driving a cart and horse to Ferryhill Market. You see we had to do this as nearly all the men had to go off to the First World War.

Dolly Whiteman

Pies And Peas

I was born at number 10 Cooper's Terrace, Thornley. I don't remember my father, I was only small when he was killed in the First World War. I had two brothers. We played mount-a-kitty, tippy cat and shuggy ring. Everyone kept something – pigeons, rabbits or a dog, and the hens used to be in the streets.

My mother took in washing and, as she grew old, she made pies and peas and I used to sell them. I had my regular customers in all the colliery streets. On pay Saturdays, I took pies to the colliery to catch the men coming from the pit. On Friday nights, I sold my pies to the men coming home in back shift.

I left school on the Friday and was down the pit on the Monday. I was sixteen when my brother was killed, he was seventeen. My mother kept me away from the pit for a month. My younger brother by one year had just started work and we were all working together when my older brother was killed. I was offered a job elsewhere but I returned to the pit.

George Soulsby

Miners ready to go down Thornley Pit in the 1920s.

The Half Way House, Thornley.

Me Daddy Was A Coal Mining Man

My father was a pitman. He was the Aged Miners' delegate for thirty years. He worked at Trimdon Grange all his life. He once went ten years at the pit and never lost a shift (this could be a record). My father was born at Thornley.

My mother had a hard life, she worked on a farm when she was thirteen years old at Marley Hill. She worked there when she was a bit of a child. And she worked at Kelloe at two farms. They both had hard lives. There were six family, four brothers and two sisters. Two brothers and two sisters died.

My father was a lovely chap and we always had income. In those days he had a garden and used to grow all sorts to feed us – spring cabbage, shallots and lettuce. Father worked at the pit until he was seventy years old.

John Egan

After A Time

I remember my father telling me of his past life. He was orphaned at ten years old and when he was nineteen he worked his passage to England from Italy. He started working for an ice cream man at Hartlepool and, after a time, he branched out on his own. He had a barrow he pushed from Hartlepool every day to sell his ice cream, and the roads were not like today. He built up his business until he employed people. He had shops in Haswell, Trimdon, Thornley, West Cornforth and two at Wheatley Hill.

During the war, my father made jelly pies for one halfpenny each because we had nothing else to sell. Things were really hard then.

There were ten of us in the family and four of my brothers were in the forces in the Second World War. It was really rough for women as most of the men went to the clubs and pubs. Women were kept down but when the war came they went into the factories, that was the beginning of better times for them, they had a little independence.

Mary Shutt (née Baldasera)

School Friday – Pit Office Monday

I was born in 1911 in the small mining village of Flint Hill, Dipton, near Stanley. I grew up in a mining household. Everyone worked (with very few exceptions) directly or indirectly at the local collieries. You were destined to go into the pits and follow your father. The girls either stayed at home and helped mother or they went into domestic service. There was no such thing as commercial or other training for girls, and the only clerical employment which a girl could get would be in a place like Consett Iron Company. And these jobs were always tied up for the daughters of the Consett Iron Company workers in any case.

At fourteen, when you finished school, you went to the local colliery. You finished school on the Friday and my father said: 'Right, Pit Office, Monday.' You would be interviewed and straight into the pit

Front Street, Trimdon Grange. The original name for Trimdon Grange was Five Houses.

on the Monday. That was me. I had twelve months work at the local colliery prior to the 1926 lockout. This was my introduction to the real hard world. Although I wasn't involved in the hard work at the coal face (working with ponies and so on) it was a bitter experience. To have to go down there and do the really heavy type of work under conditions that were not really suitable for any human being. Let's face it, I'm very clear in my own mind that coal mining is one one of the occupations that, if one could organise or run one's life without it, should not be on. You're living like a mole and working under conditions that human beings should never have to work under. Unfortunately, as a kid in those few months before the miners' 1926 Strike I realised that we were expected to do things that the horses couldn't do. We were more expendable really than the ponies that we were working with. But neither of us should have been in such a situation – horses nor men.

Maurice Ridley

Dipton Church

Bert Clarance, Consett

Wintertime at Dipton before the First World War.

SECTION TWO

GRAFTING

Young lads ready to go down the pit. Note, behind them, the wheels of a coal chauldron wagon which were a common sight around the collieries of County Durham.

Like Father, Like Son

The pits around Crook were terrible. We were working in seams of eighteen inches up to twenty inches and sometimes less, with water on the bottom and coming down on top of you. You had to lie in the seams. Lie in water. The seam I worked at Wooley was between eighteen inches and two foot high. I had to lie down all the time, often in water all day. The only time you sat up was when you came out to fill the tub, or to come out and have your bait. And there you only had four foot or four foot six at the most. For miners this was their life, lying down and coming out to fill the tub and back to lie down again.

And we weren't paid much for it either. Up until 1964 we used to get 6d a day extra for working in the wet. Sometimes you got paid extra if there was 'top water', as well, but sometimes you didn't. All you were

Two pitmen at Dawdon Colliery in 1928.
Teddy Williams (left) started work at the pit
that year.

A shot-firer drilling the coal face at Dawdon in the late 1950s.

entitled to was 6d a day, 2/6d a week for lying in water all day.

I started down the mines during the Depression in December 1937 at the East Hedleyhope Colliery. You had to fight for a job in those days, especially if you were union-minded. My father used to be interested in the unions – he was involved in the 1926 Strike and he suffered a lot through that. He travelled through County Durham and Yorkshire trying to get work. If you were involved with the union in any way in those days you were classed as an agitator. You were marked.

About 1936-37 he was able to get a job in the pit in Durham. But it was thanks to me and my brothers. When I left school we all went to the pit – myself and my brothers. My father and his brother-in-law went in the office leaving us boys outside. But the manager was adamant – he could not get a job at the colliery; there was no vacancy nothing at all. They came out of the door and the manager happened to see us three sitting on the wall.

'Who are they?'

'Oh, they're my sons – they're wanting a job an all.'

He was taken straight back in the manager's office – 'Sign on the dotted line.' My father could start the next day just because there were three sons willing to go down the pit.

In those days, if you lived in a colliery house and you had any sons they automatically had to go in the pit when they left school. If they didn't you were chucked out of your colliery house. A lot of people didn't realise this – they used to say: 'Like Father, Like Son.' They didn't realise that in those days the management controlled it all and you had to go into the pit. That was the main reason why my father wouldn't have a tied colliery house and that's why a lot of miners moved out of colliery houses. They moved into a rented house or they bought their own.

When I started in the pit, and as a young lad, when we were sitting getting our baits at lunchtime or breakfast, the old miners would tell stories about their young days and what used to happen. It was common, they said, for the overman to come and lash you across the back with his yardstick. If anybody was off the day before they had to stand to attention to see whether they were allowed to go in or not. And it wasn't so different in my lifetime. In the days gone by, they used to make slaves of the people. But I can remember when I got fined 2/6d for threatening the overman. He had threatened to hit me with a stick so I took the stick off him and broke it. I was accused of threatening behaviour and fined 2/6d. People living now don't realise what the mines were like.

Ron Rooney

Collier Lad

Your father would take you to see the pit. I was about twelve at the time and I brought back a bit of coal. I started to work a Trimdon Grange Pit when I was fourteen. I was a bit scared the first time I went down but I got used to it. I had to walk out, about a mile. On the way out, my dad stopped at a place and said: 'Do you remember when Mr Gowan was killed? Look up there that's where he was killed, at the cross gate.'

There were a lot of deaths down the pit. Everybody walked to the funerals. Everybody had their caps off and sung hymns. They had to walk to Kelloe, there was no cemetery at Trimdon. The one here was filled.

I worked at the pit all my life – 51 years. I started off as a putter. I never became a deputy. I finished off stone dusting when I was about 60.

I remember my first day at the pit. I was a trapper helping take full tubs out with the pony. I was only a child. There were two wooden doors and I had to pull them open with a rope for the men to take the tubs out. I was sitting and the putter come to me and took my lamp away. He put his lamp out. I was scared of course, I was only a child and I was sitting there in the dark, pulling the doors open. This went off for a few hours, then you got your bait, a drink of water and some jam. The men had just finished their ten hour shift. I had to work eight hours, I went down at six in the morning and came back up after 2 o'clock.

The next job I got was as a driver, I got a pony. The first pony I got was a grand little fella. They called him 'Spring'. I always remember him, he was grey. There was about half a dozen of us altogether, nice company, and we all had ponies pulling the tubs out. All the ponies had names before they came down the pit: 'Boxer', 'Whisky', 'Mottram', 'Martin' but my pony was 'Spring'.

John Egan

'Spring': Pit Pony

You are an underground Spring;
no flowers grow here,
no sunshine glows.
You are an underground Spring.

You're a dark horse
in a dark place;
your back is bruised
with coal;

yet you too have dreams
you too have dreams.

Spring into the fields,
Spring across the grass.
Spring with the children,
hear them sing!

'Spring' the pony,
Spring the trap;
Trapper-lad
Spring
the trap.

Keith Armstrong

Two photographs of men underground. The bottom picture shows Seghill Colliery and it is possible the one above is also a Northumberland Pit. However, they are included here as a reminder of Great Northern Coalfield which has now only one deep mine still working. The two counties have many mining links with men often transferring to pits 'over the border' to find work.

Frank Atkinson in his book, *The Great Northern Coalfield 1700-1900*, describes the clothing of the Durham miner:

'The Durham pitman was noted in the 19th and early 20th century for his characteristic clothing: boots and heavy blue stockings and breeches cut off at the knees and split at the ends so that they could easily be drawn over the pit boots. The hewer also wore a woolen waistcoat of natural rough felt and collarless. This he wore on top of his shirt and under his jacket while going *in bye*, on account of the cold air intake. At work he would strip to the waist and afterwards wear the waistcoat next to his skin to absorb the sweat.

J.R. Leifchild (1850) wrote of hewers: "Their pit dress is made entirely of coarse flannel: a long jacket with large side-pockets, a waistcoat, a flannel shirt, a pair of short drawers, and a pair of stout trousers worn over them. Add to these a pair of *hoggers* or footless worsted stockings, a tight-fitting leather cap, and you have the hewer ready for the pit. A pit suit costs about one pound, though some wives and daughters can make them." Cloth caps would be worn, but never a helmet until well into the twentieth century.'

An Illuminated Darkness

Miners.
Men who daily took on the fight
of defeating Mother Nature
sacrificing sweat
blood
sometimes life itself,
working in conditions that bore
no mercy
no heart
no mother.

In a world of unending darkness
lamps shone a path to follow,
beams of light guiding men to their task
or
to noises
of
creaking timber
falling rocks
danger!

Danger that had to be faced
and
survived in a stinking sewer like environment
where bait was shared with flies
and just like flies
miners lives were spent chasing the light.

Sam Cairns

Make Mining A Career

There were three men in the pits – brothers – they were great workers. The colliery manager used to say: 'If I had a dozen like them I could close the pit.' I was working on this face one day, it was about one hundred yards long and these brothers used to put the machinery up. And this particular place was only about eighteen inches high and water was falling down. So this fella was coming along. You couldn't creep, you just had to pull yourself along on your stomach, ease yourself along.

Well, he was coming along and water was streaked down his face, like streams. This was in 1940 and they had a big campaign on: 'Send your sons into mine: make mining your career.' His face came up to about a foot off mine and he said: 'Send your sons into the mine. Make mining your career!' I'll never forget that. I asked him once: 'If you had your time again, do you think you'd go down the mine?'

And he said: 'If I thought I had to go through all this again I'd cut my throat now!'

Henry Ashby

Shotton Colliery, sunk in 1840. At one time there was a brickworks nearby which produced 120,000 bricks a week.

Hewing Coals

The Consett Iron Company owned the whole countryside around Leadgate. They owned seven pits, they even had a pit in Langley Park, four miles out of Durham. They owned the whole lot – farms and everything. But because the Iron Company kept working, the pits kept working right through the 1930s. We lost some shifts but the pits didn't close.

I left school when I was thirteen and started in the pit. I started piece work when I was fourteen years old – putting. Then the very day before I was twenty-one a chap got his leg broken and I was told to start hewing the next day. So the day I was twenty-one I started hewing coals. Right up into the 1950s I was working piece rate. I hewed coals with a hand pick for $6\frac{1}{2}$d a ton up in the Eden Colliery.

When I was young I got the fancy idea of being a soldier and I joined the Territorials. I went to war in 1915 and a week after I left Newcastle I was wounded. One bullet went through my leg and came out by the side of my ankle. I had a splinter through my other foot and one near the thumb – right through the joint. When I was lying on the ground with those feet wounds I had a bullet in the behind. In fact that was the only one I felt because it seemed to go in off the bone and out again. There were eighteen holes in the greatcoat I had on at the time – so it was a bit of a close thing.

I was in hospital in Dublin for five months before I came back to Leadgate. I got £60 compensation as they decided I was alright for

Eden Colliery in the 1920s – one of the pits owned by the Consett Iron Company.

Putters and drivers at Lambton 'D' Pit in 1912. Ned Robson is kneeling second right. William Stafford is kneeling at the front, second from the left. He worked at the colliery for more than 50 years. He recalls: 'Before we went down the pit in the old days we used to meet at the top for a chat or a last smoke. Some men would be there at least an hour before they were due to go underground. There were some grand, hardworking drivers and putters in those days where money had to be earned by the sweat of the brow.'

earning a living so I went back down the pit.

I went back to Eden. I think I must have had the record for accidents there. I had cuts and broken bones. I had the same ankle that the bullet smashed broken in the pit too. I was off eleven months with that. It was the top coal that I was filling at that time. I remember I was taking the last of the coal down and the wedge was fast. So I took the pick and tried to ease it and then the whole lot came down on top of me. The coal hit me on top of the ankle. I just thought it was a bad strain and I didn't want to go to the hospital. I couldn't sleep and as soon as I'd get to sleep I'd wake up with these dreams of the stones chasing me. I'd been off eleven weeks and the X-ray in Newcastle showed that the ankle was badly shattered. The company doctor said I'd be no good in the pit any more but they wouldn't give me a light job. I had to go back and I went back to my own work. I just decided that I wasn't going to be a cripple.

Then I had a nasty gash across my knee. It was a Saturday morning shift and I'd just started. A chap had a prop under this miniature fault (where there had been small streams when the coal was being laid down). It meant that I couldn't work properly, I just touched it with my pick and the damn thing fell out and down it all came. I was sitting on the cracket. It was a terrible mess, there were small coals all over the top of the gash. So they sent for the ambulance and I arrived at the Consett Iron Company at about two o'clock in the morning. Well, the nurse who was there tried her best, poor soul. She had to clean the wound with swabs and she kept saying: 'Am I hurting you?'

I said: 'You get away. You can use a scrubbing brush if you've got one to take that stuff out. It's got to come out.' Oh it was a hell of a mess. I was sat there with this great gaping wound and there was this lad sitting beside me. He was looking at me and then the wound and then back at me. The nurse looked at him and said: 'You get out of here.' And she chased him out. The nurse stitched it up but it was that dirty she couldn't clean it properly, so after two or three days it turned septic and the stitching had to be taken out again. They had to hold the wound together with elastoplast but that couldn't draw it together enough – it left a bad scar.

Then after the Second World War a piece of stone fell between two planks and hit me over the kidney. The company doctor said: 'I'll mark you off for light work,' but the National Insurance doctor reckoned I'd recovered. So I went back to hewing.

Fenwick Whitfield

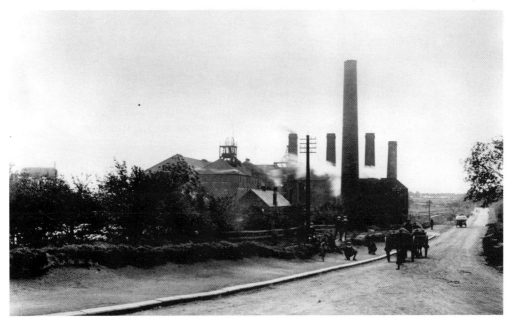

Morrison Colliery, Annfield Plain.

A team at Houghton Miners' Rescue Station in the early 1950s.

Soaked To The Skin And Black

The day I was born my dad got the sack from the pit. So I was a bad omen, he said. That was in 1931. It was the Depression and all the men got their notice. My father never had any money anyway so my parents had a really tough time.

One of the things that appalled me as a kid was the housing. We lived in Gladstone Terrace, Sunniside, a long terrace of back to back cottages, which was one of the openings leading to the pit. They were tied cottages. I can remember two old people who lived in these cottages. The old man had retired from the pit and they weren't allowed to carry on living in the house. They were turned out. I remember going to school one day and when I came back they were out on the streets. To see these people – they must have been between 65 and 70 – and the furniture that they struggled for all their lives – out in the rain had a really moving effect on me. Even at that age – I was only five or six at that time – I thought that there's something wrong that allows this to happen. All the people in the street booed when the bailiffs came. But that was it. They dragged the furniture out. Finally some neighbours took them in.

At one time my dad worked in the Hedleyhope Pit in the Deerness Valley. They never had any transport so he had to walk to the valley and back in all weathers. I can remember one night in particular when he hadn't come back after working overnight. There was a terrific storm and a hell of a blizzard and naturally my mother was really upset. I heard her stirring around so I got up and said that I'd better go out and find him. I'd only be seven years old but I was the eldest. Anyway, she went out with some others to look for the men and eventually he came in. He was absolutely clapped out, soaked to the skin and black. He just collapsed on the floor. He lay there for half an hour before he got up, and he was a big stout fella then, in his forties. He was absolutely buggered. But he went back to work next day! To do all that just for a living, and half the village were having to do this. You can imagine the impact it had on us kids.

There was a ritual my father did of spitting the jet black phlegm that built up on the fire. It was something he had to do. On warm humid

A postcard advertising coal from around 1920.

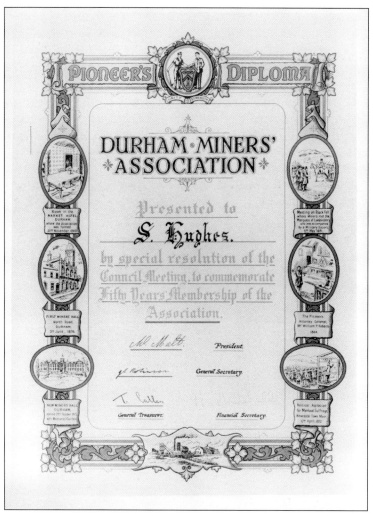

A 'Pioneer's Diploma' presented to Sam Hughes to commemorate fifty years membership of the Durham Miners' Association.

nights, when there wasn't any air, it was terrible to see him, he could hardly walk or breathe. I've heard my father say that it was bad down the pits and even with the lights on they couldn't see their hands because the dust was so bad. Eventually he was told that he'd got 25% pneumoconiosis. He died in hospital in the end. He had a hernia and the doctor persuaded him to go in. He had just got over the operation when he had a heart attack. What with his lungs it was all too much. There was an inquest and they did an autopsy. When I went down they showed me his lungs and the part where you breathe; well, it was just like a lump of coal.

Dave Ayre

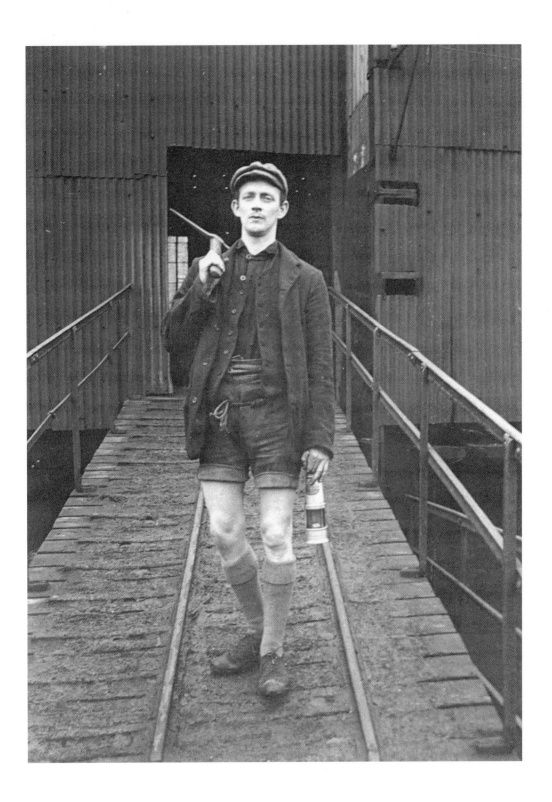

The Coal Mining Man

My daddy was a coal mining man,
Yes, my daddy was a coal mining man.
From dawn till night and night till dawn,
He worked the mine till his life was gone.
My daddy was a coal mining man,
With props of wood these men of iron
Worked like hell down this goddamn mine,
With shovel and pick they moved stone and coal,
Black as night down this stinking hole.
My daddy was a coal mining man.
Breaking props and creaking stone,
A fall of stone and some men groan.
With clouds of dust and choking grit,
Daddy worked hard down this hellhole pit.
My daddy was a coal mining man,
'A way of life,' it was often said.
'One way to earn a crust of bread.'
Daddy took bad and could work no more
But it taught me one thing, and that's for sure:
I would not be a coal mining man.
I worked in pits and that's very true
But shovel and pick were not my scene.
I left in search of pastures green;
Daddy died, a broken man with shattered dreams,
A numbered token in some pit-gaffer's screams.
This was his life and he carried the can –
His reward for being a coal mining man.

John Iddon

The Pit And The Dole

My grandfather was a Cornish miner and he came to Coxhoe when the mines were closing in Cornwall. There was a dispute at Coxhoe at the time – that's why they were sent for, as blacklegs – and my grandfather and the others refused to start. The people of Coxhoe took them into their homes until the pits started again. If they hadn't been taken in they would have starved. In those days, you'd have to be dying before the parish would give you anything.

My mother didn't want me to go down the pit. She took me away on Saturday to an uncle of hers who was going to train me as a saddler. When we got there, he was as deaf as a stone. In those days they had a big trumpet that you had to shout down. Well, I thought, I'm not stopping here. My mother went back and I'll bet before she was home in Tursdale I was at Dawdon with my grandfather. And I was down the pit on the Monday. My mother didn't know for a while but eventually she found out I was in the pit and she said that if I was to be a miner I had just as well go down the pit at Tursdale nearer where we lived. So that's what I did.

A lot of the lads were very kind to the ponies. They'd get very attached to them, particularly if one was a good worker. They'd pinch carrots and turnips from the fields on the way to work for them. Some of the lad's mothers used to give them apples. You'd tell your mother, you know, about the pony – how it was a good pony – and she'd say: 'Oh, take an apple for the poor thing!' My mother was always giving me apples – one for me, the other for the pony.

In the timber yard at Seaham Colliery in 1947. Left to right: Jack Hays, John Williamson, Ernie Rowell, Brian Corkhill and Harry Mortensen.

Thornley Colliery, Vesting Day, 1st January 1947.

Right through the Depression years I remember lads with their ponies. Sometimes on the main drive ways of the pit they would ride the ponies out – flying out like cowboys. The overman would be standing there with a riding crop covered in chalk and he'd tap you on the shoulder with it. All those who had a white mark would be fined.

There was an awful lot of bullying down the pit. I could get young lads to work for me and the overman used to say: 'George I don't know how the hell you do it but these lads like to work with you.' I was kind to them you see. I didn't bully them around. Some of the overmen down there were real bullies. One of them had been a professional wrestler and he was a big man but he never frightened me. I used to say to him: 'Anytime you're ready Jack. I'll have a go at you.' Some pits used to set men on like that. Big strong men who would frighten people, bully them.'

In the 1930s people were afraid to strike with so many out of work. The managers used to say to you: 'If you're not satisfied you know what to do ... You can pack it in now if you like.' They weren't long in telling you. Back-answer the boss and you were sacked.

George Bestford

The Apprentice

I was an apprentice fitter & turner to Geo Burnsides Ltd, Mill Pit, Shiney Row – Mining engineers and manufacturer of 'patented safety boring apparatus. They used to search and tap-off water or gases from old mine workings. It was an antiquated factory, more like a very large blacksmith's shop with machine tools. The family owners were of pit stock and had the business handed down to them from inventor grandparents. The 'Boss' was Geordie Matthews and the foreman was his brother Tucker who sang like a nightingale and had a mouth like a sewer. On my first day there, as a boy of fifteen, he made it his first task to teach me every swear word he knew.

One day, I was working on a centre lathe and my overall sleeve was caught in the running workpiece. My arm was dragged into the machine and my shoulder slammed against the slowly-revolving twenty inch chuck. I was saved by my own sheer strength (by then I was a hardened eighteen-year-old youth). The chuck was driven by a wide flat belt; I threw all the weight I had against the chuck and grabbed it with my free hand. For a moment I held the monster in a kind of head-lock, and it saved me. The belt skidded then slipped off the pulley and the chuck stopped.

My overall sleeve was shredded to the shoulder and my arm and

Sixteen-year-old Brian Lister at work at Geo Burnsides Ltd,· Mill Pit, Shiney Row.

chest were badly scrubbed and bruised. Tucker treated me with the only thing he ever stocked in the first-aid box, sal-volaite. He sent out for a pad of lint and sticking tape. When it came I was given it to dress myself, which I did.

I have a Burnsides catalogue. There's a picture of me, about sixteen years old, assembling part of a safety boring machine. I'm kneeling down, dressed in boiler suit, cap, heavy boots and thick muffler. There's a leather 'finger-poke' on my right forefinger; a result of an accident with a milling machine cutter. I'd been lucky not to lose my finger that time. On another occasion, the same lathe that grabbed my arm almost removed my ability to father children. There was this long square threaded lea screw, it ran lengthways along the front of the machine and you had to lean across it while you worked. You had to remember not to get too close to it! It was strength, fuelled by mega-panic that saved me that time. I fought like a madman and swore at that would have made even Tucker blush. Again, I escaped with strained muscles and shredded overalls. Geordie, when he heard, was sufficiently interested to come out of the office for a snigger. 'Thou should be more careful. That's the best friend thou's got young 'un.'

Brian Lister

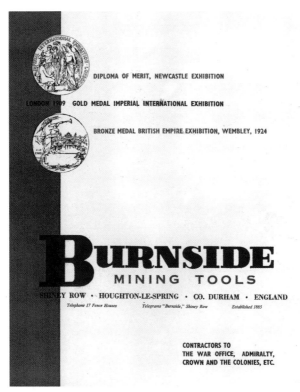

An advert for the mining engineering company.

The Old Ovens

I first came to Fishburn in the early 1920s, when I was four years old. My parents bought a house at 14 Park View and my father worked at the Coke Ovens. He was a gas regulator and worked three shifts, year in, year out, regardless of Bank Holidays – the work never stopped until the 1926 Strike. I believe he got three holidays a year. Once every three weeks he worked a double shift from 2 pm Saturday until 6 am Sunday. It was my job to take his bait down to him on the Saturday night, usually a hot meal in a basin and a fresh can of tea. It was a bit frightening walking down the pit yard for a small boy but I got used to it. Then every three weeks he worked another double shift from 6 am Sunday to 10 pm Saturday, and this time it was Sunday dinner that had to be taken. All this, of course, was to bring about the change of shifts and to enable the men to have a weekend off from 6 am Saturday to 6 am Monday.

The 'bait cabin' was a brick alcove at the end of the ovens where the favourite seat on a cold day was the back wall next to the ovens which was always hot. Here, also, in a small cubby hole, the tea-can was left to keep warm.

There were fifty ovens in a straight line terminated by a large chimney. The ovens were filled with coal from a loader running on a track above, and each oven was closed by a door, front and back, each door being sealed round the edge by a sort of clay called 'daub' manufactured in a 'pug mill' at the end of the ovens. When each

Fishburn Colliery.

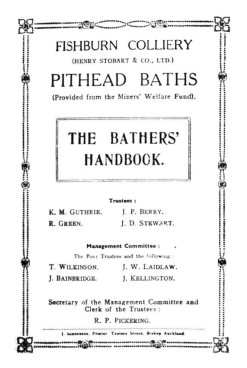

The cover of Fishburn Colliery
Pithead Baths, Bathers' Handbook.

Miners at bank around 1920.

individual oven was ready for pushing, this was done by a ram, which ran on tracks, the length of the ovens being moved to each one as required. The doors having been raised, the hot coke was pushed out on to the slopping bench, through a framework carrying jets of water called the unquencher. The coke was further quenched by means of hoses and when cooled was loaded into twenty ton trucks at the bottom of the bench by men known as coal fillers who each used a multi-pronged fork, known as a 'gripe'. The gases from the ovens were taken to the scrubbers where many by-products such as tar, benzole and sulphate of ammonia were obtained from them. A lot of gas was wasted, which could have been used for industry or for domestic purposes, and this always escaped into the air from a tall pipe at the end of the ovens. When this was ignited, the flame could be seen from several miles away. Incidentally, this posed quite a problem during the black out in war-time when the flame had to be extinguished.

In the early days, there were no pit head baths and all the miners and coke oven workers came home unwashed. We had no bathroom until later years and my father bathed in front of the kitchen fire in a zinc bath tub.

George Gargett

Medomsley Branch Co-operative Store. Often at the heart of many colliery villages, 'The Store' was where all goods could be bought. They used to say it catered for all your needs – 'from the cradle to the grave.' A dividend was paid on all purchases and even today most customers still remember their 'divi' number from years ago.

An advert for the Ryhope and Silksworth Industrial and Provident Society.

Pit baths in the 1960s. The introduction of pit head baths brought a welcome relief to miners' wives.

A Miner's Wife – A Full-time Job

My father worked down the pit but he would never have his back washed. Never. It used to be filthy. His theory was that if you washed your back it weakened it. My mother used to go on to him about the bed clothes being filthy, about his clothes being filthy, but no he wouldn't wash his back. So she had to wash more sheets.

Being married to a miner was a full-time job for a woman, especially if she had sons who worked at the pit too. My mother had sons and lodgers! In those days it was considered the duty of the wife to be up to see that her man's pit clothes were warmed by the fire and his breakfast was ready. She'd just get him out to work and somebody would be coming in – bath in front of the fire, poss-tub out (his pit clothes would be filthy and sopping wet), in with the clothes, wash them and dry them. It's marvellous how they survived really; and my

Dawdon Miners' Hall in Mount Stewart Street which was officially opened in 1912.

mother was just a little woman.

The men didn't give their wives all their wages. They used to have what they called 'keepy back', money which they used to hide from their wives. Men used to get up to some amazing tricks to hide the money. Men coming home from the pit would have to bath, take their clothes off and keep a half gold sovereign in their hand. They'd wash themselves with their hand in a fist. They'd hide money in their carbide lamps and all sorts of things. There'd be hell to pay when the woman found out but, in those villages, you weren't a man if you didn't have some 'keepy back'. You were the boss of the house.

If the husband died, the woman was expected to go into mourning. If she went to the pictures nine months after the funeral the talk would start. 'Did you see Mrs So and So. Her man's not cold yet.' The women weren't supposed to go anywhere. They had to stop the clock, turn the pictures to the wall and have white handkerchiefs with black edges round. All of this done by the woman. After a funeral the men would be standing in the yard, looking at their watches to see when it was opening time. And they'd be in the pub everyday after that. But if the woman went to the pictures, nine months or a year after, she'd be the talk of the place.

Women weren't supposed to drink or go into pubs or clubs. Any woman who went to the club was considered to be a floosie. But my mother used to like a drink of beer. She used to like to go out and mostly on a Friday night she'd slip over for a drink. She'd go across to the pub but wasn't allowed into the pub itself. There was a little ducket place on the side where the women would stand and have a glass of beer. Maybe they'd take a jug of beer home. On a Friday night, my mother would say to me: 'I'm going across for a glass of beer – don't tell your father mind.' I wouldn't tell him. If he got to know, Good God, there used to be hell's flames around the house. He was a big fella.

George Alsop

Thornley Colliery. Sinking began on 9th January 1834. The sinkers were a group of Cornishmen who were eventually evicted from the village for rowdiness. The colliery closed in 1970.

Are You Working?

If you went to a dance and met a boy the first thing you'd ask was: 'Are you working?' If you could get a boyfriend who was working you knew you were quids in. When I started going out with one particular boy my father said: 'What are you doing with him? He's not working. You want nowt with him. You want somebody who's working.'

In a mining village there was no work for girls. A lot of women would have loved the extra work but there was none – not like the mill towns. Some women would take in washing, but in a colliery village there was no prosperous people either. Maybe a doctor or the colliery manager. My auntie used to take in washing and she would do a fortnight's washing for four people. She would wash, starch and iron four people's clothes for a fortnight for ten shillings.

One family in Chopwell had three daughters. They never married and they used to make quilts and clippie mats. They would work all

A delivery cart in a Durham village. Note the brasses hanging from the horse.

week around this big frame and every week they would deliver either a mat or a quilt. People would be paid £3 a week. Out of that they'd have to buy the wool for at least a pound which would leave the three of them £2 for a week's work.

Girls when they were fourteen used to go down to Newcastle in service. They used to get half a day off every fortnight. Every Wednesday in Chopwell you would see the girls coming home and then on every other Sunday afternoon. They used to get about ten bob a week and their keep. The two girls next door to us were in service. There were no washing machines and so they had to do all the washing. I know those two used to hate it. They were always leaving and coming home and their mother would go mad. She was always saying: ' You want to get yourselves a boyfriend.' Someone who would marry them to take them off her hands. One day her daughter, Florrie, said to her: 'Mother there's two million surplus women in the country so somebody has to go without a man.'

'But aye,' she says, 'bonny hard lines when two out of my family have to go without.'

I would have hated to go into service. I was in dread of it. If I hadn't had to look after my father, I would have had to go. As it was, I got one of the very few jobs in the village for a girl. I was favoured to have that job. I used to clean the picture hall in the morning and take the tickets at night, for 12/6d a week.

Hilda Ashby

Women's Work

When I was a girl the only work for women was domestic employment. In those days you'd hear girls say: 'I'm going to London to service.' They'd be going to be a domestic servant in one of the big houses in London. In my married life I've done any number of jobs, in between having children. I had my fourth child when I was thirty-eight. I've worked nearly all my married life with different jobs – I liked to do something. I've worked in a fish shop, I've been a domestic help, I've gone round with butter and eggs, and I've been a barmaid at the RAOB Club. At the club, I used to see men come in night after

Outside the Single Aged Miners' Hostel, East View, New Seaham in the late 1930s. Left to right: Paddy McCartney, Emily Wright (one of the maids), Mr Dobbin, Barbara Bleasdale (caretaker) and Matt Yore.

night, spending money on beer, and I know for a fact that their wives and bairns didn't know which way to turn. I used to think that was awful. When we were hard up, George, my husband, used to do without but at the club men used to come in, pass pound notes over the bar and stand there drinking beer and their bairns were running about in bare feet. It used to sicken me.

There was some work in Chopwell but the majority of work in the area for women was at Prudhoe Hospital. A busload of women would leave the village every morning. I started working there when I was fifty and I stayed there eleven years, until I retired. After I had been there a while I wished that I'd gone there years before instead of the bit jobs I'd done before that. At Prudhoe, I used to think I was doing a job that was worthwhile. You were looking after somebody that wasn't capable of looking after themselves. If they were in pain, you could ease their pain. You could care for them. And, in the end, it was better money too. But I liked the work and I liked the company. I made a lot of friends at Prudhoe.

I wasn't keen to go in the beginning though. Everyone kept saying: 'Wey, gan to Prudhoe, man.' You know, as an auxiliary nurse. Well, I'd heard about Prudhoe and the dirty jobs there. I thought: 'I'll never go there. I'll never be able to do that job.' But, in the end, I applied and I got on. All the way on the bus, on my first day, my insides were

Taking home sea-coal from the Blast Beach at Seaham.

churning. The others said to me: 'Just put up with it for two weeks and when you get your first pay it will be lovely.'

Six pound odd, that was my pay. And we had to work hard. We had to do all the domestic work, scrubbing the floors, everything – we hadn't any time for the patients. On one occasion the sister, myself and another nurse were on our knees scrubbing the floors when these people arrived unexpectedly. They were somebody important from some important place. The sister said: 'You'll have to excuse me.' She had to wash her hands before she could shake hands. This man said: 'But you are the nurses here, what are you doing this for?' So they went up to the office and the next week they set the domestic cleaners on. By the time I left, they were earning as much as the nurses and I thought: 'It must have been slave labour with us the first few years; they were getting their work done cheap.'

Vera Alsop

Silksworth Colliery. This site, like many former pits, has been transformed since the colliery closed. Now a ski-slope, lake, running track and sports fields occupy the land.

Men And Women

The real people who really suffered when we were unemployed were the women folk. Scratting and scraping and having to do all the cooking. The miner's home had its own bake house. The oven next to the fire was a little bakehouse and, however difficult it was, the home-made bread, white or brown, the stotty cakes and the tea cakes were laid on. It was the wives who put in the sixty and seventy hours a week, week in and week out. And the dedication in doing what they could with so little is something the modern generation probably cannot understand. The women were really wonderful, almost without exception, they had to cook and keep things together, without any of the modern helps and it was amazing how they did it. I was lucky in the sense that my mother was very good at this. But there was an enormous amount of self-help as well.

Tom, along our street, had a big allotment and he kept pigs, and when a pig was killed … bonanza! The day a pig was killed (it was all done locally by the local butcher) you had your pork chops for the weekend, and black puddings of course.

It was marvellous how the mums were able to sustain big families on very little, they were very resourceful indeed. Chancellors of the Exchequer! – Those women could buy and sell them.

The men weren't involved in any of the so-called domestic duties. How shall I put it? Essentially the duties had been laid out beforehand; the miner or the iron and steel worker did his stint and was responsible for his wife and family. But the domestic side was completely under the control of the mother with the help of any daughters that might be

A coal bill from 1934. Coal was 75 pence per ton, in today's money. It is small wonder the miners were so badly paid.

there. Interference wasn't wanted and very rarely given. Mother was in charge domestically, 100 per cent and the man's role was as a breadwinner, wherever it was and there was a clear division of labour. Very, very clear division of labour. And the pattern had been set generations before, you grew up and you had to conform. A male who involved himself too much in the domestic side was unfortunately looked upon as a bit of a sissy in the community.

The workingmen's clubs were another part of this division. These were the places where the males, generally at a weekend sometimes during the week, used to go for their 'crack', discussion and drinking. The social life of the mining community, for the males, was centred around the club or the miners' welfare institute. And the club was a complete male preserve. No females. These clubs had very often been started in this area by lodge officials and others. The clubs did a great job from the point of view of providing good quality beer, cheaper than the big private concerns could or would provide. The people who formed them, established the same rules at the club as operated in their own household. The division of labour was the same. A social club is for men, a place of work is for men; the women's role is in the home. And the pattern was established and it followed itself through into the social life. A great pity, but we've learnt how to do it much better since.

Maurice Ridley

Dean and Chapter Colliery, Ferryhill.

Two views of Wearmouth Colliery – the last deep mine in old County Durham which closed in 1993.

Horden Colliery, 1902.

For The Last Time

For the last time
men
leave their place of work
ride the underground manset
walk the windy road to the shaft
ascend in the cage
hear the sound of forced air
hand tokens to the banksmen
replace self rescuers and lamps
take off dirty smelly clothes
shower in the block where so much dirt is washed away
and where so many jokes were played
on unsuspecting soap eyed mates

For the last time
men
change at their lockers
making themselves presentable for the outside world
and for the very last time
men
walk out the gates
never to return
surplus …
to requirements.

Sam Cairns

SECTION THREE

SAD TIMES, HARD TIMES

A commemorative postcard for the West Stanley Colliery (Burns Pit) Disaster. An explosion on 16th February 1909 killed 168 men and boys.

The Trimdon Grange Explosion

Extract from the sermon preached by the Rev Oates Sagar, MA, Deaf Hill-Cum-Langate

Turn we now to that event which was produced among ourselves those tokens of sorrow so vividly described in my text. On a sunny day, in a remarkably summer-like February, when the birds (early returned) were singing cheerily in the sky, that happened, which, to many among us, turned the light of the sun into darkness, and caused sounds of lamentation and bitter weeping to rise up to heaven. At half-past two o'clock, on the afternoon of Thursday, the 16th of that month, an ominous sound was heard at Trimdon Grange and even for some distance around, which has been described as like the sound of a boiler

Trimdon Grange Miners' Lodge Banner.

Deaf Hill Terrace, Trimdon Colliery.

explosion. Anxious eyes were turned toward the mouth of the pit, and smoke and ashes were seen rising from the Harvey shaft, and then dismay and apprehension filled the minds of all. Too soon it was known that an explosion of gas had taken place and it was felt that many lives must have been sacrificed. The sad intelligence spread rapidly through the neighbourhood and multitudes flocked to the spot. Help came speedily from all directions. Mining engineers and their officials; miners in great numbers, with their agents, came to tender their services; and the surgeons of the locality were there, ready to discharge their necessary duties. Men were found willing to descend through the choking stithe into the mine, and the greatest exertions were made to discover the extent of the disaster, but it was some time ere this could be done. Meanwhile, it was found that the area of the explosion was not confined to the Trimdon Grange Pit, but that the deadly gas had forced its way through a connecting passage to the Kelloe Pit, which is worked by the same owner; and the miners there were compelled to flee for their lives. Six men, however, perished there: some of them gallantly led by the manager, H.C. Schier, ME, also died in an attempt to open the communication between the mines.

It was some time before it was known how many lives had been lost at Trimdon Grange. The living were brought to the surface in a few hours, the less exhausted of their number bravely waiting at the shaft till the others had been brought to bank. Nine of them had been saved through the presence of mind of a veteran miner, the back overman,

J. Soulsby Snr, who had kept them out of danger. The last of the saved was brought up shortly after nine o'clock, and it was felt that those who were still in the pit could not possibly have survived what was found to have been a most destructive explosion. Out of 93 men and boys who had gone down into the Harvey Seam that morning, only 26 were saved.

No exertions were spared by night or by day, and no expense was begrudged, in opening out the pit. Many volunteers ran great risk in performing this task, and in recovering the dead. Early on Monday morning the last body was carried home. It is supposed that all must have died in a very few minutes (some say five), and thus sufferings could not have been prolonged.

One man, J. Errington, was found with a boy on each arm, and another laid over him. He had evidently been trying to save them, and had lost his life in the attempt. One of the 26 saved, the fireman, P. Brown, was so dreadfully burnt that he died on the following Tuesday, after great sufferings. He was ministered to by members of the Primitive Methodist body. The engineman, H. Ramshaw, and his assistant, a boy, W. Taylor, were among the saved, but the former had been blown by the force of the explosion some distance from his engine. On recovering his senses somewhat, and learning what had happened, he exclaimed, 'Whatever shall we do?'

The boy's reply was, 'I think thou had best pray.'

Such was the first thought that arose in the mind of this boy, and such, we may well believe, must have been the first thought of many who perished, if they had time to think at all. Many of them were only boys; out of 68 who perished at Trimdon Grange, 31 were under 21 years of age. Many of them, it is consoling to know, were Sunday scholars; whilst of the older ones, some were Sunday School teachers and members of churches. I myself have personally known many of them for years, as well as their friends, and they were very dear to me. I have had some of them in my own Sunday School, some I have prepared for confirmation, and other clergymen others; while not a few of them have worshipped with us in various ordinances of the church, both here and at old Trimdon. And now, within the short space of one week, they have disappeared from our view, and their places shall know them no more. 'My heart is distressed for you my brothers!'

And what shall I say by the Word of the Lord to those who mourn the untimely removal of their beloved ones, whose voices were lift up in lamentation and bitter weeping on that day of fear and trembling, and on days of suspense which followed. There were some, indeed, whose grief was too deep for tears, and whose dumb sorrow reminded one of the poet's line:

'She must weep, or she will die.'

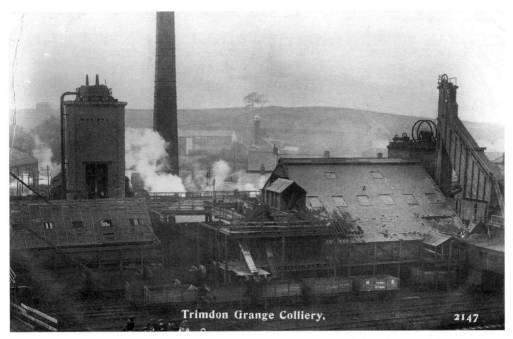

Trimdon Grange Colliery. The darkest day at this pit occurred on 16th February 1882 when 74 men and boys lost their lives after an explosion.

The Trimdon Grange Explosion

Oh, let's not think of tomorrow lest we disappointed be.
Our joys may turn to sorrow as we all may daily see.
Today we're strong and healthy, but tomorrow comes a change,
As we may see from the explosion that's occurred at Trimdon Grange.

Men and boys set out that morning for to earn their daily bread,
Not thinking that by evening they'd be numbered with the dead.
Let's not think of Mrs Burnett, once had sons but now has none –
By the Trimdon Grange Explosion, Joseph, George and James are gone.

February left behind it what will never be forgot;
Weeping widows, helpless children may be found in many a cot.
They ask if father's left them, and the mother hangs her head,
With a weeping widow's feelings, tells the child its father's dead.

God protect the lonely widow and raise up each drooping head;
Be a father to the orphans, do not let them cry for bread.
Death will pay us all visit. They have only gone before.
And we'll meet the Trimdon victims where explosions are no more.

Tommy Armstrong

The 74 men and boys who lost their lives in the Trimdon Grange Explosion Thursday, 16th February 1882

Buried at Trimdon

February 19th:

	Age		Age
James Boyd	13	Joseph W. Burnett	23
George C. Burnett	19	James W. Burnett	17
William Burns	35	Michael Docherty	14
Edward Spencer	19	Joseph Dorman	14
Thomas Dorman	13	Patrick Durkin	13
Joseph Hyde	23	William Jefferson	18
George Jefferson	14	John Williams	31
William Jennings	17	Michael McHale	21
John McHale	16	Thomas McHale	13
Samuel Richardson	17	George Simon	16

February 20th:

	Age		Age
Frederick Bowen	23	William Bowen	16
Henry Burke	39	Richard Dawe	20
John Edmunds	13	Dave Griffiths	19
Michael Hart	45	Cornelius Jones	18
John F. Jones	38	Ralph Mercer	18
Henry Miller	24	Thomas Priestly	29
Andrew Smith	23	William T. Stubbs	31
George Wigham	28	William Williams	31
John Wilson	33		

February 21st:

	Age		Age
John Allison	19	Thomas Clark	24
Matthew Day	13	George Dobson	26
John Smith	26	Thomas Peat	21
Thomas Pryor	26		

Buried at Kelloe

February 19th:

	Age		Age
Robert Edwards	17	John Errington	33
Thomas Horden	56	William Maddrell	40
Christopher Prest	35	John Ramsey	26
Frank Ramshaw	17	William Robinson	34
Ralph H. Robinson	17	George Slack	21
Robert Soulsby	60	Jacob Soulsby Jnr	27
Richard Thwaites	27	John Wilson	15

February 21st:

Thomas Hunter	37	William J. Hyde	26
Henry Joyce	16	Enoch Sayer	18
George Richardson	29		

February 23rd:

Peter Brown   60

February 29th:

Jacob Berriman	33	John Douglas	13
David Edwards	16	John Hughes	29
William Parker	16	Thomas Sharp	42

Buried at Cassop-cum-Quarrington

February 19th:

Thomas Blenkinsopp 37

Buried at Shadforth

February 20th:

Robert Maitland   40

February 21st:

Matthew French   13

Buried at Croxdale

February 20th:

Herman Carl Schier 23

THE VICARAGE, KELLOE.

The Buzzer

When there was a fatal accident at the pit, the buzzer gave off three sharp blasts and everyone appeared at their doorways. Men in the opposite shift hurried down to the colliery to find out what had happened and see if there was anything they could do to help. In the early 1930s, it was usual for the pits to work two or three shifts per week. Everyone waited at six o'clock to see if the buzzer blew the 'pits off the morn', then sighed with relief when it didn't.

There were people much worse off than we were. Men came begging for pennies, some with one arm or leg. They were war heroes and this is what they came back to. I remember a whole family, father, mother and two children, standing huddled together in the middle of our street, degraded in ragged clothes with rough sacking on their feet tied with coarse strings. Youths of fifteen and sixteen years old went carol singing for pennies, their clothes in rags with shoes falling apart. My mother brought them into the house and sat them by the fire with a mug of cocoa and bread and jam. They were from Hartlepool. They'd walked, calling at the colliery villages as they went. The collieries were the only places where there was any money, little though it be.

Gladys Bromilow

Remember The Forgotten

In the shadow of a mine
stands a graveyard
where lies
countless boxes of memories
in a field full of friends
over-shadowed by the spirits
of the men who
laughed
cried
lived
and died
thus becoming
another box of memories
in a field full of friends.

Sam Cairns

Carried Home

When I was a very young, a chap was killed in the pit. I remember them bringing him home; of course, in them days there was no pit bath. They put him on a stretcher and carried him home as he was, black, dead. They put a blanket over him. There were no street lights then, one man had a torch at the front, another man had a torch at the back. About six men carried him. His wife was screeching with crying. She took the poor fellow in. She had to wash him. I was about eight or ten then, I remember it well.

John Egan

Down the pit at Thornley.

Looking For Work

All the villages had places where men would stand at the corner in a bunch and talk and have a cigarette. You'd have about two draws out of it and then out. You'd light it up about five or six times to make it last. A weekend treat in those days would be to walk up to Consett and walk around the market place looking in the shop windows. You couldn't afford to buy anything. Just look in the windows and walk home.

In those days, if you'd been on the dole for so long you had to go on what they called the Tribunal. A man would come down to the house to interview you. You went up before the Tribunal and he would say: 'Where have you been looking for work?' If you weren't looking for work they'd suspend your Dole or stop it altogether. Well, looking for work then was absolutely farcical. We used to get a bicycle and go all around the district and everywhere you went there were hundreds of men sitting around with no work.

Anyway, we had to go in front of this chap to explain. He'd say: 'Where were you on Monday?' and you had to have the name of the place where you'd been looking for work. 'Where were you on Tuesday?' he would ask and then go through the rest of the week. Then he'd try to trip you up. 'Where were you on Tuesday again?' If you couldn't remember or give the same name, he'd scratch your name off and stop your Dole. So I had a little square piece of cardboard with a name on it for every day of the week. I used to carry it inside the cuff of my jacket. So when they asked me where I had been I'd look out of the corner of my eye for the answer. They never tripped me up.

You'd go to places and ask: 'Is there any chance of a job here?' and they'd look at you as if you were daft.

We thought of these people, the Tribunal and the Means Test, as the enemy. I can remember the time when there was a Relieving Officer (this was before the 1930s) and he would look around your house and say: 'That sideboard, you don't need that.' You had to be absolutely penniless before they let you have anything.

Many a time during the 1930s I'd look at the rent man with dark thoughts in my mind. But I never did anything nor did other people, there was very little robbery during that time but I'm sure there would be now if people were reduced to such a state. People today just wouldn't stand for it.

Henry Ashby

'The Doggy Boys' – a group of men in the Ryhope/Silksworth area in the late 1890s.

Miners at Silksworth in the 1890s.

Seven And Six A Week

My father worked down the pit until he was fifty and he had rheumatism, he couldn't work any more. He was on the sick and his sick benefit was 15 shillings a week. After he'd been on it for a certain time it was reduced by half to 7/6d a week. That's all my mother had to live on for the rest of her life – seven and six a week. He had a few hens and a couple of gardens. Without that he wouldn't have survived.

Henry Ashby

Jobs For Some

I have hazy recollections of a soup kitchen in the village and the distribution of boots to really needy children. Girls at school, especially some of those from the largely poverty-stricken Catholic families, often wore a white pinafore over their clothes. These pinafores were probably the only ones they had and were, apparently, worn day in and day out until they were ragged and had to be replaced by a new one. Girls from better off families wore gym tunics. The boys were divided into similar categories; the poorer ones had jerseys and the better-off ones suits. I must have been somewhere in between, wearing a jersey underneath a reefer jacket! I did have a suit for Sundays, though.

Women footballers in 1926. It is likely the game was held to raise strike funds.

In those days of the Depression, there was one well-established routine, every Tuesday and Thursday was dole day. There were young men who had never done a day's work before they were 21. There were middle-aged men who never worked again, even during the Second World War, as if their bodies had shrunk and their spirits too; so that they weren't ever again physically or psychologically capable of a sustained effort.

For all the greyness of unemployment, or intermittent employment, the spectrum of material circumstances stretched from dire poverty to modest wealth. The extreme of poverty was pinpointed by one family who occupied a tall house at the very eastern end of the village. My father was a bookies' runner for a short while and, having to call at the house in question, he saw at first hand the slum-like conditions under which the occupants lived. I never went with him on those occasions, but with a voice with a mixture of sorrow, despair and pity, he used to tell us of the bareness of the rooms and the matching emptiness of the people living there. The husband had been in the Army, had a prison record and was married to a feckless wife. There were children and the one who, almost more than anyone else symbolised the family, was a boy who was never seen outside of the house until he was almost ten. He used to stand at an upstairs' window looking up along Front Street in full view of anyone coming down. When he did start school, the reason for his seclusion became obvious; his legs were wasted and he had to wear callipers to enable him to walk. He had a cynical, bitter, look, quite out of tune with his years.

At the other end of the scale were the village capitalists, best typified perhaps by a builder. He lived in a superior type of house in Front Street, with front and back gardens. He possessed a cart and his wife and daughters wore fur coats (as some of the village teachers did).

Just along the street from this 'posh' house, was a small terrace of better-class houses of the bungalow type. One of these was occupied by the manager of the 'Little Pit' a mile away from our village, which was closed and its site cleared before the Second World War. I used to go with my mother to the house of this colliery manager. It was during these visits that I helped to make 'proggy' mats which were such a feature of the mining community. It was strange to go into a house with a hall and several rooms, in contrast to the one that we lived in with its door leading straight from the foot of the stairs into the front garden.

Jack Goundry

A 1920s soup kitchen. J.N. Pace, in his book 'Ryhope & Silksworth' recalls: 'During long strikes the miners' first priority was to ensure the children did not suffer unduly. With meat bones begged from local butchers and vegetables from their gardens, nourishing hot soup was served daily from tin baths to keep the children fed.'

Believed to be during the 1921 strike, these miners are seeking usable coal among the waste beside a colliery railway line.

In hard times, the men who had mined the coal often had to dig for their own on the pit heap.

The opening day of the Miners' Institute at Pelton Fell.

Sick Money, Public Relief And Rent Money

We were in one room when we first got married. It was a room we sub-let off a council tenant. Then we went into a cottage and we had a downstairs room and a bedroom upstairs. I had to cook on a little fire in my bedroom. We had two babies while we lived there, they were just nineteen months apart and I had both of them by the time I was twenty. At that time my husband, George, was just on a small wage at the pit. By the time I paid my room and rent and furniture, I was lucky to get 3d worth of pie meat for the Sunday dinner. George got no pocket money, sometimes he would say: 'Have you got 3d to spare?' If I had, he would go to the local institute and play skittles. If he won, he would call at the fish shop and bring fish and chips and share them. He would get fish and a pennyworth of chips for 3d.

Every winter, he got pleurisy pain and he would be off work for weeks. We would get 15 shillings Lloyd George (sick money) and 5 shillings rent money to live on.

My granny helped me as much as she could but there was a limit to what she could do. She said I would have to go to the Public Relief. I was frightened to go but she said there wasn't anything to be ashamed of as it came out of the rates, and, if the King could live off the rates, why couldn't I? I went once but I never went back.

We were in that room for about four years before we got our first house; a council house which we had for twelve years. Then we moved down Mill Road for an extra bedroom. We had three daughters then and one had asthma and had to have a room of her own. At that time, we couldn't have a colliery house but it came that we could. So we moved into Mersey Street and then Humber Street. So we moved a bit but always in the village of Chopwell.

Vera Alsop

A Militant Village

Chopwell was known as a militant village; it got itself a reputation for that. The lodge banner played a big part. It was the only banner with Karl Marx and Lenin on it. This banner is now in the Community Centre at Chopwell. Then there was the street names – Marx, Engels and Lenin Terrace. The village was also very active in the Friends of Russia after the Revolution. This is where the 'Little Moscow' idea came from. I was once sent a letter from down south in the 1960s. It was addressed to 'Lodge Secretary, Little Moscow, Durham' and I got it. The village was always staunch Labour – left Labour. I remember during the George V's Jubilee in the 1930s they raised the Union Jack on Blaydon Council Offices. It didn't stay long. A chap called Poskitt climbed up and pulled it down.

DERWENT STREET, CHOPWELL 1237

Chopwell was out on strike nine months before the 1926 Strike began. There was a local dispute over the prices in the pit. The men were advocating and struggling for an increase in the prices. The only offer that they got from the management was that they were prepared to give one group a rise, but there would have to be a reduction in other parts of the pit – robbing Peter to pay Paul. They struck nine months before the General Strike started. I'd just left school at the time. I was fourteen years of age and the main thing I can remember was the way in which the Council of Action organised things in the village for the children. Bits of dances, sports days, foot-running, sack running and that sort of thing. We used to participate. It was all organised to entertain the young ones.

And then there were the soup kitchens. Everything was so organised that at least the children got something to eat. There was one thing that they were all bent on and that was that they weren't going to see the children either go hungry or without heating.

The women folk used to make great sacrifices. They used to do the cooking and looking after the bairns, seeing that they got their proper share and they used to see them to school. It was amazing to see the organisation behind it while they were so restricted. It used to be a good feeling that you were all one family.

The men started little drift mines. They found some coal down in the wood and they got permission to mine it. They used to organise it properly with proper shifts, deputies and safety regulations.

CAR LINES, CHOPWELL. 1245.

Chopwell Colliery banner with the portraits of Keir Hardie, Karl Marx and Lenin.

Another thing that sticks in your mind is the blacklegs. They used to be escorted backwards and forwards to the mine. I remember the processions very well. The whole village would be standing around with the lads humming the death march. There were hundreds of people there escorting the blacklegs and there used to be heavy struggles.

The Council of Action really organised the village during the 1926 Strike. The leading trade unionists in the village used to meet regularly in the workingmen's club. Most of the activities were organised from the club rather than the trade union branch meeting. The facilities of the club were put at the disposal of the Council of Action committee. They'd sit, have a pint or two, and plan out all the activities. The Council of Action really controlled the village. If a lorry came in with some produce or stuff on the wagon, they used to say: 'What is it?' and

A closer view of Chopwell Pit.

they used to give them a permit to go to the shop and drop it off. If they didn't get a permit into the village they couldn't come in. The Council negotiated with the shop, asking that they allow people to have credit on the guarantee of the union that the people would pay it back monthly when they got back to work. And this is what happened. Some people sharked of course, some of them went away, but the majority of them conscientiously went to the shops and said: 'Tack that off the back.' This was how we all survived. Without this credit we wouldn't have survived.

The Council of Action organised all these things. But in the end the Strike was defeated and the leaders were blacklisted. My family was blacklisted. We didn't get a start in the pit until 1928. Some never worked again in Chopwell. Following the Strike, it was just a continuous struggle; the miners had to go back on less wages and longer hours. The struggle had to start all over again.

George Alsop

A group from the S.E.A.M. Campaign – 'Save Easington Area Mines – in the 1980s. They were at the forefront of the miners' campaign during the 1984-85 strike. One of the vital tasks the women performed was working in an Easington kitchen providing meals and food parcels for up to 700 miners and families five days a week.

The saddest day at Easington occurred on 29th May 1951 when an explosion killed 81 men at the pit. Two members of the rescue team also lost their lives.

The Easington Disaster

At the pithead, in the dawn,
rescue teams look old and drawn.
Sickened by the last vain search,
where two men died to save a corpse.

Weeping women, mangled men,
can we face it all again?
Yet, we must, for, if we strive,
perhaps we'll find just one alive.

Down this grim, blast-shattered mine,
bodies sprawl where our lamps shine.
Once strong men, once eager boys,
lie broken like discarded toys.

Our hopes have gone, our tears we've shed,
there's nothing down here but the dead.
Eighty three's the final toll;
the endless, bloody, price of coal.

Fred Ramsey

SECTION FOUR

ENJOYING OURSELVES

Hetton Juniors AFC, 1927-28 – Winners of the Durham County Junior Cup, North Eastern Divisional Cup, Hetton Junior League, Northern Echo Cup and semi-finalists of the Blind Institute Cup. Back row: G. Liddle, S.R. Davison and W. Dobson. Third row: Lowery, G. Patterson, J. Rodham, D. Donkin, S. Davison (chairman), R. Kendrew (assistant secretary), J. Richardson and R. Walton. Second row: C. Smith, T. Shipley, T. Taylor, S. Bagley (captain), H. Tennet, G. Gibson, J. Smith, P. Bartley, J. Howe and W. Usher. Front row: W. Jennings, N. Blunt, G. Marsden, T.W. Davison (secretary), J.F. Bell (president), F. Dixon, J.T. Shaw and R. Craddock.

Games

Quoits was common, the young men playing it on the village green with quoits and hobs probably belonging to our local pub, the Cross Keys in Esh. Schoolboys used to improvise, though, using a roughly rounded stone as a hob with flat stones, of the type used to top dry stone walls, as the quoits themselves. The village green provided other sources of pastimes too. The soil was clayey and it was possible to dig out lumps of it sufficient to form them into a box-shaped object with an opening in one of the smaller ends. A lid was put on, again of clay, so as to leave a gap at the end of the of the top away from the first hole. Bits of paper were stuffed inside of this rather pointless contraption to be set alight, hence its name – a 'puffer'.

Our village was a good place for the 'gliders'. Those four-wheeled bogies favoured by children as a plaything and means of transport, because most of its main street was a gradual slope. One boy, whose father had been a farmer but had gone into the haulage business, owned an especially posh glider. It had superior wheels and steering and even brakes. This young man would give his friends a free ride down to the bottom of the village, but would make a small charge to any other child who fancied a run. His budding business sense also extended to another of his activities. In an outhouse behind his father's bungalow, he used to hold shows, using a small projector. Once again, he used to have 'private' free shows and other shows at one halfpenny per head.

Jack Goundry

Tennis courts at the Welfare Park, Horden.

Leek growing has been a popular pastime in the coalfields for many years. Here are two judges inspecting some fine examples. Expert Seaham leek grower, Fred Gleghorn, is on the right.

The card for Trimdon Feast Races, 27th August 1921.

Childhood Games

In 1929 we moved to a much bigger house with a staircase. My father built a wash-house in the yard. We played shops and concerts in there, the toilet was the stage. I remember some of the rhymes we chanted whilst playing skipping ropes: 'On a mountain stands a lady', 'Who she is I do not know', 'All she wants is gold and silver', 'All she wants is a nice young man', 'Carry a bucket of water for my lady's daughter', 'Her father's a king, her mother's a queen', 'She is the first maiden I've seen', 'Stamping grass and parsley', 'Buttercups and daisies', 'One in a rush, two in a rush' and 'Come see my ladies dancing'. We played games like: 'One old Jew just came from Spain', 'There came three gypsies riding', 'Tippycat', 'Jack shines the maggi', 'Hoist the flag', 'Hitchy bays' and 'Buttony and marbles'. Everyone had a penker which was a marble much bigger than the others. You played with that one and, if you lost the game, you paid up with a small one. We had rhymes for Halloween too: 'Riding on a broomstick', 'Riding on a moonbeam', 'Riding on a cabbage stalk', 'Tonight is Halloween, when all the witches can be seen, some in black and some in green, hey ho for Halloween'.

The carnival was the main event of the summer. It lasted a whole weekend in August. The streets were hung with bunting and flags, the shop windows were decorated, the shops that were double-fronted had one window dressed in patriotic theme – the Royal Family, Union Jacks, ribbons and royal regalia with Britannia with her trident as a centre piece.

The procession took place three times: Saturday afternoon at 2 pm and Friday and Monday at 6 pm, led by the brass band and the carnival king and queen in an open carriage. There were competitions for the best dressed house too. The window and doorway were decorated and, under the window outside, there was a small tableau of dolls. I remember some of them: a hospital ward with beds and patients, a table with a lamp on it, and a nurse sitting at the table. There was a Teddy Bears' Picnic and Santa Claus filling the stockings. These were surrounded by a fireguard or a small wall of bricks. It was a treat to walk the streets to see them.

When I was twelve, I used to go to Mrs Roper's Farm to help her in the dairy after school. I helped her to strain the milk and skim it and clean the dairy out, feed the geese and hens and collect the eggs. A little song she sang was: 'Hicky, Bicky, Dicky Bean, now the dairy's nice and clean, you're the fairest youth I've seen, so now we'll go a courtin' o!' She bought me my first pair of silk stockings. I treasured them and only wore them for chapel on Sundays.

Glady Bromilow

A rag time band in 1926.

Workers At Play

If we had Dole cards, we could go to the pictures twice a week for twopence. We used to walk from Tursdale to 'The Gaiety' in Ferryhill and spend the afternoon at the pictures. That was a good entertainment – twice a week. We forgot all our troubles watching cowboys and Charlie Chaplin. It was a two hour show and we'd walk back for tea. That's how most of us learned to read. In the picture house everybody would be reading the words out to people who couldn't read.

People used to walk together in age groups, and you'd walk for miles. I've seen games of football last all day. We were lucky in Tursdale, we had a leather ball which lasted a long time. I've seen twenty a side. People used to come along – young men, young ones – 'Which way do I kick?' At other places, people used to sew their caps together or blow up a pig's bladder. If you were a good footballer – or a cricketer – you could always get work in the pits. In Tursdale you were set on if you were a sportsman. We had sixteen horsekeepers at Tursdale – all professional footballers. The trainer for Durham City was

The Hippodrome, Thornley, opened in 1912. At one time, every colliery village could boast places of entertainment such as the the Hippodrome. In 1938 the Ritz Cinema was opened. In the days before television the population looked for cheap entertainment provided by the Hippodrome and the Ritz.

one of the overmen, the undermanager was one of the directors. One of the horsekeepers told me how he'd sleep for hours down the pit before a match. A lot of men didn't mind. They liked a good worker or a good sportsman.

George Bestford

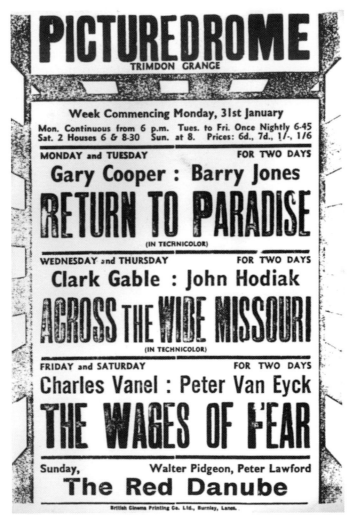

An advert for the Picturedrome, Trimdon Grange, from the 1950s. The film 'The Wages of Fear' is unusual for being the first foreign film with subtitles to be given a wide release in Britain. Audiences throughout the country were gripped by this exciting French thriller which the told the story of a group of men driving explosives through a South American jungle to extinguish an oil-well fire.

Handball

I was born in Sixth Street, Horden, against the handball alley. When there were matches on there our old man used to look after the alley. My mother used to make the tea for the men that were playing and I used to take it in. I saw all the big names, all the big stars that were playing handball then. When the ball got brayed back, all the heads of the people watching nodded backwards and forwards. One man was knocking the ball back up the alley and it went over the top and they found it down behind the church. It went right along Seventh Street so it'll tell you how hard he was hitting the ball, and the skin on those balls was above an inch thick. The men's hands, when they'd finished playing, seemed to be all split right across the palm. They used to put cobbler's wax on it and still keep playing.

Ralph Porter

Harraton Colliery cricket team, 1955. Back row: T. Huscroft, B.F. Humble, A. Dean, W. Charlton and R. Habron. Front row: A. Louth, C. Brown, D. Scott, J. Colpitts, F.G. Swan (Colliery Manager) and W. King.

The victorious Crook Town players celebrate winning the FA Amateur Cup in 1954.

Amateur Greats

I can remember when Crook Town had as big a support as some of the Football League teams. The year they beat Bishop Auckland was tremendous. At Wembley they played a draw, twos apiece, and then played another, twos apiece at Newcastle. Then they beat them, one-nothing at Middlesbrough. What I remember was the friendly atmosphere. Although they were at loggerheads with each other, after the match at Wembley we drunk together in the pub. They were shouting abuse at each other, but drinking together in the same pub. At matches, you would get away fans from Romford and other places and you used to mix with them. They would stop until late in the night and you would say: 'Well, what about coming home for tea?' After the match, whether you lost or won, you used to take them home – some would take two or three.

Ron Rooney

Silksworth Colliery Welfare football team in the late 1940s. At this time the colliery welfare teams dominated local football. Successful pit teams in the decades after the Second World War included: Easington, South Hetton, Horden, Shotton, Seaham, Dawdon, Eppleton, Boldon, Ryhope, Murton, Langley Park, Thornley and Blackhall.

The Soviets

Chopwell's football team was called the 'Soviets'. They wouldn't let them join the league under that name. They said they would if the name was changed. But they wouldn't change the name. It was a good team as well. Lads, hand putters from the pit, came straight out and played football. They never got washed sometimes. They used to go on the field black. Some of them went away to play League football.

George Alsop

The Institute

Each village had its Institute with a billiard table in a room. Billiards was only 3d a game and it lasted twenty minutes. Or there was dominoes, chequers and sometimes chess. Men used to meet there in the evening. I used to play a lot of billiards and the dream was that I would get locked in so I could play billiards right through the night for nothing.

Henry Ashby

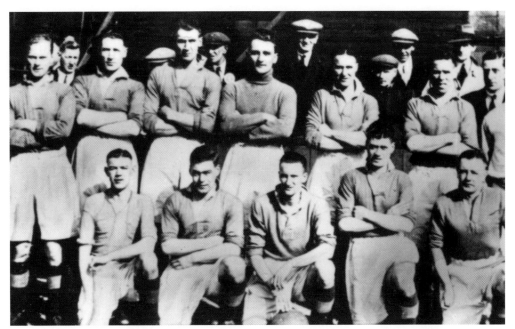

Horden Colliery Welfare F.C. in the 1930s. Back row, left to right: H. Duff, B. Bradford, E. Kirtley, J. Hickman (captain), E. Reay and S. High. Front row: J. Robinson, A. Dunmore, W. Cook, F. Laidman and V. Murphy.

Blackhall Colliery Welfare F.C. also in the '30s. Back row, left to right: R. Donnelly, A. Parker, P. Bartley (captain), J. Jarps, W. Jones and G. Elliott. Front row: J. Wilson, C. Ferguson, W. Rochester, E. Catton and W. Bradshaw.

Academy Of Football

In his book *Hotbed of Soccer* Arthur Appleton called County Durham the nation's finest football nursery. Local villages provided so many quality footballers that many had to leave the area to find a professional club. He pointed out that in 1933 there were 341 players from County Durham on the books of Football League clubs.

The following are just a few of those who left the area to find fame in the 1920s and '30s.

Pelaw-born Ron Starling played for Washington Colliery before going on to win an FA Cup winners' medal with Sheffield Wednesday and England caps.

New Washington's Will Furness was spotted by Leeds United playing for Usworth Colliery in 1928. He went on to play for his country.

Tom Graham joined Nottingham Forest from his hometown club Consett Celtic. He played for both England and the Football League.

Birtley-born G. Maddison signed for Spurs as a youth but after a brief stay in the capital found fame as Hull City's 'keeper.

J. Holliday was signed by Middlesbrough from Durham amateur side Cockfield but soon moved on to Brentford.

Tom Holley was the son of the famous George Holley of Sunderland. He left Wearside to join Barnsley.

Thornley's Tom Nicholson, English Bowls Champion, and team.

A moment of thought during a bowls game at Silksworth Colliery Welfare Park in the 1970s. Bowls is one of the many traditional sports of the colliery villages.

A Wind-up Gramophone

When we were first married I had a little cabinet gramophone on legs with a winder. It was the first one to come into Hamsterley Colliery. It had been my granny's and she said: 'It's yours when you get married.' Well, when I brought it up to my husband George's house they couldn't get over it. My mother-in-law thought it was great. She couldn't get over it. But now you've got speakers all over the houses; music centres and other things. We've seen a lot of things change.

Vera Alsop

Shotton Colliery Silver Model Prize Band, 1924.

Street Betting

Apart from clubs and pubs, there were more personal pleasures like gambling. In the 'old days' street betting was, of course, illegal so the bookies' runners operated furtively, though known to the police. I had it from one such runner that police awareness manifested itself in quite different ways, depending upon the temperament of the constable involved. One, for example, would warn the runner when the 'super' was due on his rounds. Another, on accosting a runner whom he knew to be carrying bets, would say casually on passing him: 'Mine's in the usual place.' But another, of a quite different type, and in another village, would tell the runner to approach the bookie for a backhander, or else.

Jack Goundry

Trimdon's Salvation Army Band.

The Sun Inn Revisited

The last drink was served at the Sun Inn in Bishop Auckland some years ago and then it stood empty. Finally, it was demolished and moved bit by bit to Beamish Museum. It was a surprise to me to see it as it has been reconstructed. I had expected it to be as it was – old and shabby and not very respectable. Not the sort of place you would take a girl for a drink. Instead everything had been done up to look neat and tidy, the way it must have looked when built the first time. The paint and brickwork are now clean and fresh looking. I wished it had been open so that I could have gone in to see if the inside had changed as well.

I would also have liked to see if the beer tasted any better from the last time I drank there, when a pint cost about half a crown. That would be when I was a teenager.

It was not the sort of place to go in and mix easily unless you were part of the regulars, and many of the regulars had big reputations as drinkers and fighters. Many of them were hawkers, and a lot of their talk was about horses and the horse fairs like Appleby, which a stranger would find difficult to join in.

A newcomer would have to be very careful in what he said in case he upset someone and landed himself in trouble. It was the sort of place where troublemakers go, and wouldn't think twice about hitting out at you. They were the sort of people who stuck together and if one started trouble you could guarantee the rest of them would join in, especially if their friend was getting knocked about. Trouble was especially likely to happen on a Thursday, because it is Market Day and the pubs stayed open longer on the afternoon.

Three or four years before it closed a landlord started to improve it by cleaning it up a bit inside, but, as with many other small pubs in Bishop Auckland about the same time, things came to an end. Even the houses in the area have now disappeared in redevelopment to make way for roads and a bus station. After the Sun Inn was moved to Beamish, flats were built on the site where it used to stand.

Philip Gill

Beamish Hall, Beamish, :8⣋2⣋

Beamish Hall, Beamish – for many years part of the famous Open Air Museum. Beamish Museum was first opened for an introductory exhibition over twenty weekends in 1971. The following year visitors were able to see the site for the first time. Since then the Museum has gone from strength to strength becoming one of the favourite visitor attractions in the North East.

The former Bishop Auckland public house, the Sun Inn, is one of the buildings in the award winning Town which shows a typical street of the early 1900s. As well as the pub, there are houses, Co-op shops, bank, solicitor's office, dentist's surgery, newspaper office, sweet shop and garage. These buildings have been restored brick by brick to their former glory.

A day trip from a colliery village to Finchale Abbey (Priory) in the late 1890s. In the days before convenient transport, outings such as this was probably the furthest these people ever travelled.

CLIFF STEPS, BLACKHALL ROCKS. 2364.

The cliff steps at Blackhall Rocks. Another popular day trip destination for colliery folk.

Freedom Night

In small mining villages during the 1920s and '30s there were rare occasions when people could throw off the yoke of the masters and forget their troubles for a while. Such a village was mine and a rare occasion was the Durham Big Meeting.

The Friday night before the Saturday, the atmosphere of subdued excitement that had built up during the week, gave way to unrestrained boisterousness that infected young and old. The working members of the family would gather at the union rooms, which was a pub, to watch the lifting of the banner. At this point, as a warming exercise, the band would play a tune. The effect of hearing the music was to send most of the young 'uns running towards the band. A crowd of shrieking, laughing lads and lasses, hopping up and down, knocking each others' caps off. We were free to go in with jerseys with holes in, short trousers (adult trousers cut down), dirty faces and legs, stockings sloggered over boots, and join the marches.

The march had started by the time I reached the milling group behind the banner. I was grabbed by a cousin, who dragged me through the crowd of men, saying: 'Thee da's waiting for thou.' When handed over, my cousin was off to join his mates.

My dad firmly grasped my hand as I was hopping up and down like a jack-in-the-box. His first words to me were: 'Pull thee socks up and put thee cap on straight.' This I did, hopping from one foot to the other using my free hand. Looking up at him, I said: 'Are yu carrying the banner this year?'

Looking down at me he said: 'Not this year lad.' Seeing the

Men in fancy dress at the Gala in the 1950s.

Seaham Colliery Banner on the racecourse at Durham in the mid 1920s. In front of the banner are some well-known Seaham men, including Lodge Officials James Hoy, Joe Cutting and John Alexander. Also in the photograph is John McCutcheon, author of the famous book 'Troubled Seams'.

expression of disappointment on my face he bent down and said: 'Th's gannin' to Durham.'

Gripping my hand, we jostled our way to the front so as to be walking under the flapping banner. I was surprised to see our Jack carrying the banner. I knew now how and why I could go to Durham. Sticking my pigeon chest out in pride, I walked behind the banner with my dad.

After walking a short distance, I said: 'Dad, our Jack's wobbling about. I thought he was strong. Our Frank's helping him to keep the pole up.' Giving my arm a sharp tug, which pulled me to face him, pointing his finger at me, he said: 'Th' sees o'er much for a young 'un. He's had a drink or two, so say nowt to yu ma.'

To us young' uns, the banner was a piece of cloth on which was painted a picture on both sides. When older, we would appreciate the art and craftsmanship that had gone into the making of the banner. The words on the banner had no meaning to us young' uns but, in years to come, we would learn the hard way; learn also of the deaths, starvation and cruelty men and their families suffered, were still suffering at the time of these memories, so that the pictures and words would, for future generations of miners, become reality.

As the marchers moved from street to street, the older lads and

Dawdon Banner and Band on Elvet Bridge in the 1950s. Leading the way in fancy dress are Sam Hughes and Billy Wood.

lasses linked arms and zig-zagged from one side of the road to the other. They couldn't dance the full width of the street as the pavements were crowded, mostly with women, young and old, with clean pinnies or aprons. Wives holding the bairns up to see their dads, some shouting at husbands with young 'uns in tow to 'look after them'. Mothers shaking fists in the directions of sons, shouting at them not to spend all their money tonight. To be caught with your arm around a lass, unless officially courting, was trouble in the shape of a brother or the heavy hand of a parent across the lad's ear. But not this night.

Whether it was the thought of the beer waiting for them at the pub, but the speed of the marchers increased as they got nearer to the starting place, the pub, where the banner would be stored ready for tomorrow.

The excitement over, the young 'uns were dashing off home with dads, straight home or else. I hurried straight home to ease my hunger, which was satisfied with the home baked pies, this particular Friday night's treat. Then a bath and off to bed.

Arthur Reid

The 1926 Gala

During the early weeks of the strike the Durham Miners' Gala was held. Usually, of course, the Gala is held in Durham but in 1926, for a number of reasons, it was held at Burnhope. I walked there with other young locked-out miners and our parents, and it was my first real experience of the leadership that was really in charge of our struggle. I should say that the speech of Arthur Cook, who was the secretary of the miners' union, affected me for the rest of my life.

There were at least thirty thousand miners at the meeting. It was a magnificent turnout and, of course, they had to get there the best way they could and many of them walked from goodness knows where. We walked five or six miles, but many of the people there that day walked much further. But that didn't matter. Even though it wasn't held in Durham, it was recognised that this meeting taking place at Burnhope was to be addressed by the leadership of the miners and the politicians within the labour movement who were supporting us. For any ordinary trade unionist it would have been a crime not to be able to go. I mean you just automatically had to go because you were in the midst of the struggle.

Maurice Ridley

The Proletarian Display

An extract by Rough Lea-born novelist Harry Heslop (1898-1983)

When Bob Smillie and Chiozza Money came to address the first Durham Gala after the war, we carried our banners and escorted our

The Murton Lodge Banner is paraded through Durham on Big Meeting Day.

brass band with the deepest of reverence. In those days, the Gala was a sight for all men to witness. The enormity of the proceedings outstripped the imagination. Perhaps it was the setting that lent privilege to the proletarian display. Maybe the vast mustering of the colliery tribes, under the arches of the massive, brick-built viaduct that spans the yonder part of the city and carries the great railway, grants a piquancy to the subsequent proceedings. The boomings of the drums provoking the attention of the tribes and then the double tap which unleashes the brazen sound into an almost dreamlike unreality and sets men and women marching. Repeated almost two hundred times the resulting noise and slashings of colour provoke an almost spiritual

Labour Party leader and Miners' leader shake hands at the Miners' Gala in the 1980s.

Neil Kinnock and Arthur Scargill lead the way during the day of the Gala.
Denis Skinner is to the left of the Miners' leader.

aura that hangs like a proud destiny over the immense beauty and rich colour of the city.

The narrow streets forced an intermingling of marches and amused watchers. The crossing of the bridge over the Wear, that cowers like a coward within the ample shade of the great cliff that holds both the Castle and Cathedral up to the arms of God, was always a strain lain upon the carriers of the banners. The passing over the bridge, beneath the lovely scene evoked by tree-clad heights and glory-crowned buildings, always evoked for me some strangely murmered benediction wailing softly into unreality. There is nothing so magnificent within Christendom that compares with the loveliness of Durham Cathedral. Ordinary men must have built it but they must have been men filled with an extraordinary vision, for they left it, where it stands, encompassing, and encompassed by, its own earth rising upwards to immortality like a prayer passing the lips of a woman suckling her babe.

It is this Cathedral which has softened the harsh lines of the men of coal every time they have ventured into the city to listen to the orators. It is never forbidding, never minatory. It watches them marching to their venue, and when all is over, it beckons them back to their possession of their own lives. It is this half-church, half-refuge, that softens the spirit after the pains of unremitting toil and tempers the thundering of exhortation into crooning and beliefs.

The Dawdon Band marching along Queen Alexandra Road, Dawdon, in 1954. At the front is bandmaster, Stanley MacDonald.

Leo Chiozza Money removed his hat and stood up to speak to us on that day. The Gala had been a revelation to him, to such a degree that he was still astonished and bewildered. Bob Smillie sat smiling. Both had been fighters at the hearings of the Sankey Commission. Bob could understand the little man's bewilderment. And when Money had breathed his prayer over the vast crowd, 'God bless you all,' Bob reached over and patted him on the shoulder. Bob was a showman in his own right. He stood up and accepted the acclamations of the concourse. While it boomed over the city, and stilled the rowers in the boats on the lovely breast of the Wear that flowed nearby, he mounted a chair and when the noise had died away he began to speak.

Durham Big Meetin' Day

by Johnny Handle

They hold it in July, me boys, it's caaled Big Meetin' Day,
And for weeks and weeks beforehand, the miners save their pay.
The lodges have their banners, and each one has a band,
And the beer it flows like water, so we drink aal we can stand.

The polises close the roads up, they torn the cars away
For Durham is stoppened off, me lads, upon Big Meetin' Day.
The bandsmen aal assemble with their horns so blindin' bright,
And they blaa from in the mornin' till gannin' hyem at night.

The crowds they aal gather an' the bands began te play.
They march up to the Meetin' groond, an' Ryhope leads the way,
An' then we hear the speeches, an' they tell us what gans on,
Of wor hopes an' troubles, an' where the government's gannin' wrong.

Noo, as they speak o' present times, me mind wanders back
To work an' unions long ago when masters broke yer back.
Aa min me aad grandfather, an' what he said te me.
Of how they fought te get their dues, how unions came te be.

They broke the yearly bond an' the masters crooked scales.
They fought the blackleg miners from Ireland and Wales.
When torned oot o' their houses, wey together they did stand
And they formed the Miners' Union that's known throughout the land.

So we've got better conditions and better money too,
We've taen the pits unto worselves to see what we can do.
But when we've paid the masters off with interest rates as well,
We'll show them coal's not gannin' back; we'll have a tale te tell.

Wey, with the speeches over, the folks aal torn aroond
Te happins an' te bars an' pubs where fun can be foond.
There's roondaboots an' shuggy-boats an' dodgem cars se fine,
An' lads an' lasses carrying on, an' havin' a good time.

Noo there wes some gannins-on, Aa think they should think shyem,
Aa blushed mesel when Aa went oot inte the back lane.
But then Aa thowt: 'Noo, shut thy gob, thoo's done the same thysel.
For if thoo thowt when thoo was young thoo'd have a tale te tell.'

Noo, Aa's suppin' beer from dawn till dark an' mind, Aa had me sup,
For Durham comes but once a year, an' it takes some savin' up.
Although there's fights an' arguments, Aa think we have a right
Te lowse worselves oot once a year, an' end up gettin' tight.

So if ye come wi' me next year, just get you pockets lined.
Fetch the missus an' the bairnies if ye have a mind.
We'll hear the band an' speeches too, an' spend maist o' wor pay,
But we'll have oorsels a bloody good time at the Durham Big Meetin' Day.

Fishburn Lodge Banner, miners and their families at the Durham Miners' Gala.

The Banner Comes Home

Gala Day was always a big day in Chopwell. The Friday before Big Meeting Day everybody used to bake plate pies with meat in for people to take away with them. At seven o'clock in the morning, they'd march with the banner around the village and then up to Blackhall Mill and to Westwood Station. They'd all get on the train there and go to Durham. At night, everybody who hadn't gone to Durham for the Big Meeting Day would wait around the street for the banner coming back. They would get off the train and march all the way up with the band playing. It was always a big thing. People would say: 'Wait till the banner comes home.'

Hilda Ashby

The Banner – Our Emblem

The banner, our emblem for numerous years
Was carried in triumph or laden with tears.
Every Big Meeting Day, up Thornley Main Street,
Along with the band, we danced to the beat.
Marching through Durham with pride, cheers and hopes,
Borne by the poles, the ribbons and ropes.
On the racecourse, it was stood down to rest,
Oft-times with black crepe adorning the crest,
A symbol of sorrow that had happened that year
As fatal disasters did often occur.
A colourful picture of every hue,
Biding the time till the service was due.
Then to the cathedral for thanksgiving prayers,
For shedding of fears, of worries and cares.
Thoughts of past struggles, upmost in minds,
Undaunted, united as comradeship binds.
It hangs now with honour in our village hall,
No longer requested to answer the call.
The banner – our emblem, we so frequently saw,
In regal procession we see it no more.

Gladys Bromilow

Thornley Lodge Banner at the Gala in 1956.

The Contest – A Tribute To Thornley Band

They sit around in horse-shoe style
Instruments ready all the while
They watch the man in uniformed hat
With baton raised, no silly chat.
The work's all done, rehearsal gone,
It's now that they have practised for.
The bandmaster keenly scans the score,
Down comes the baton they've been waiting for.
They play their hearts out
Because they know the other bands are formidable foes.
'Beethoven's works' – the test piece played,
Opening butterflies soon allayed.
Unison, then a great solo
A cadenza, to make the performance grow.
Loud applause at the end
Greets them wildly like 'Amen'
Of course, they won
With points in hand
No others could touch the Thornley
Our silver prize band!

Ben Murray

Whitworth and Spennymoor Town Prize Band.

*A charabanc trip
leaving from the
Colliery Inn, Pelton Fell.*

HORDEN CLUB.

*Horden Club – before
and after a fire. Known
as the 'Big Club', it was
built by the local coal
company in 1906. It
was burnt down in
1910 but re-opened two
years later after being
rebuilt by its members.*

Acknowledgements

Thanks to all those people who helped compile, edit and produce the following Strong Words/Durham Voices/Northern Voices publications, extracts from which make up most of this book.

Hello, Are You Working? Memories of the Thirties in the North East of England, Strong Words, 1977
But the World Goes on the Same. Changing Times in Durham Pit Villages, Strong Words, 1979
The Way I See It, Fred Ramsey, Strong Words, 1980
What Price Happiness? My Life from Coal Hewer to Shop Steward, Dick Beavis, Strong Words, 1980
Horden Miners, East Durham Community Arts, 1984
Durham Voices Magazine No 1, Summer 1984
The Last Coals of Spring, Poems, Stories & Songs by the Women of Easington Colliery, Durham Voices, 1985
Where Explosions Are No More, The Trimdons in the Words of Local People, Durham Voices, 1988
We Are The Valley, Stories, Pictures and Poems, Durham Voices, 1988
From Fissebourne to Fishburn, Fishburn Past and Present Told in Stories, Poems and Pictures by Local People, Durham Voices, 1989
From Pit Wheel to Green Field, Thornley Past & Present in the Words of Local People, Durham Voices, 1990
One Fell Swoop, Pelton Fell Past & Present in the Words of Local People, Durham Voices, 1990

Thanks also to:

Sam Cairns for permission to include poems from his booklet *The Heart Lives On*.
Andy Croft for contributing 'The Proletarian Display' by Harry Heslop.
Johnny Handle for permission to include his song 'Durham Big Meeting Day'.
Brian Lister of the National Association of Writers' Groups for the loan of Geo Burnside Ltd catalogue.
Gary Miller of 'The Whisky Priests' for the loan of photograph and permission to use his lyric *This Village*.
Bill Robson, the demon barber of North Shields, for the loan of family photograph.
Trevor Williamson for access to photographs and information from his East Durham Archive.

St John's Church, Sunnybrow. The church was built in 1885 and demolished in 1979.

Bibliography

Arthur Appleton, *Hotbed of Soccer*
Frank Atkinson, *Life and Traditions in Northumberland and Durham*
Frank Atkinson, *The Great Northern Coalfield 1700-1900*
Eileen Hopper, *Easington The Way We Were*
Mike Kirkup, *Eyewitness: The Great Northern Coalfield*
Tom McNee & David Angus, *Seaham Harbour, The First 100 Years 1828-1928*
William A. Moyles, *Mostly Mining*
J.N. Pace & Andrew Clark, *Ryhope and Silksworth*
Trevor Williamson, *Images of Seaham*

Horden, The First 100 Years 1900-2000

Picture Credits

Freda Allen, Marian Atkinson, Lavinia Barstead, Carol Birkbeck, Fred Bond, John Carlson, Ian S. Carr, Anne & Jim Curry, Fred Gillum, George Hoare, Brian Holden, Jack Howe, Sam Hughes, John G. Humble, Olive Linge, George Nairn, J.N. Pace, Derek Williams and John Williamson.

The People's History

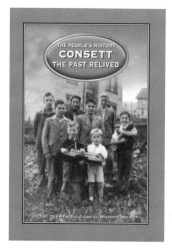

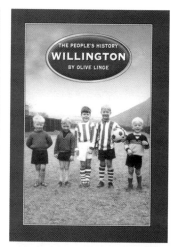

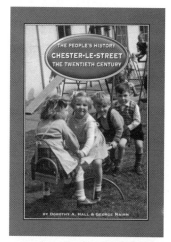

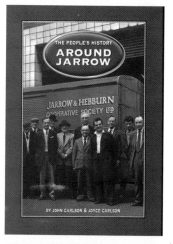

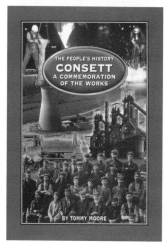

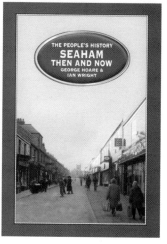

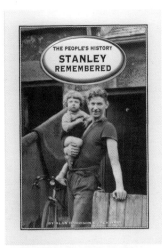

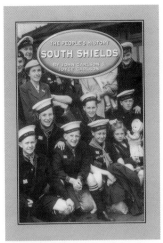

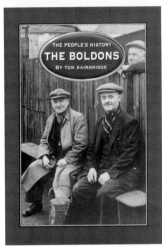

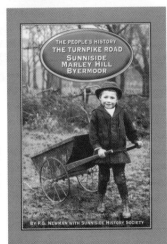

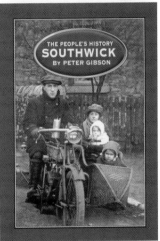

Also available: Bishop Auckland … Brandon And District … Houghton-le-Spring … Penshaw, Shiney Row, Philadelphia & Newbottle … South Shields Scrapbook

Low Row, Easington Village. On the far left is the Methodist Chapel opened in 1885. Four doors down is the Shoulder of Mutton – one of several pubs surrounding the village green.

The People's History

To order a book in The People's History series send
a cheque or postal order to:

The People's History Ltd
Suite 1, Byron House
Seaham Grange Business Park
Seaham, County Durham
SR7 0PY

All books are £9.99 and postage and packaging is free.

Cheques and postal orders made payable to The People's History Ltd.